BUYING AND FITTING SADDLERY

In the same series

Right Way to Ride a Horse
Right Way to Keep Ponies
Practical Horsemanship

BUYING AND FITTING SADDLERY

by
Karen Bush and Sarah Viccars

PAPERFRONTS
ELLIOT RIGHT WAY BOOKS
KINGSWOOD, SURREY, U.K.

Made and Printed in Great Britain by
Hunt Barnard Printing Ltd, Aylesbury

ACKNOWLEDGEMENTS
Anita Scoular, Dilys Thompson

CONTENTS

LIST OF ILLUSTRATIONS

INTRODUCTION

The money spent on buying a horse or a pony is only a preliminary to further expenditure; after this follow bills for feed, stabling, vets, shoeing – and of course, saddlery.

A glance in any equine magazine or shop window should be enough to confirm immediately that most items of saddlery are expensive. Obviously it is not desirable from the horse owner's point of view to spend money on equipment which in the long term could prove unnecessary or expendable, so the action and purpose of any piece of saddlery must be thoroughly understood if benefit is to be gained from using it. In addition, especially when buying secondhand saddlery (as many people are forced to do in order to keep costs to a minimum) it is very easy to be misled as to its quality and condition, so caution must always be exercised.

Financial considerations put to one side, safety and comfort for both horse and rider through the correct fitting of tack is vital, especially since many problems can be traced back to the misuse, abuse, or simply ignorance of, much equipment. Often the solution lies in simplifying the saddlery used rather than adding to it. Physical or rider problems should also always be checked out as a possible cause; a horse or pony which leans on the bit, for example, could be due to teething problems, or the rider's bad hands, not necessarily the tack. For a novice horse owner, the most successful combination of saddlery is nearly always the simplest possible. A snaffle bridle and general purpose saddle, provided they fit properly, should be perfectly adequate for most activities. However, on progressing in ability, the rider may wish to specialise in a particular sphere of equitation, or a problem might arise which requires a greater understanding of equipment.

This book is intended to explore these ideas, and to provide a guide to correct use and fitting of equipment in common everyday use.

Items carrying a proprietary brand name are not included. There are far too many of these to list, making it impractical to do so, especially as new brand names appear on the market each week. Additional information about such pieces of saddlery which cannot be found in this book can be obtained from the manufacturers, and should be fitted and used in accordance with their instructions. However, the many modern materials which have recently been introduced into the manufacture of saddlery are fully covered, as well as the more traditional ones.

1

MATERIALS

Many of the materials used in the construction of tack and horse clothing are natural – *leather* being the most obvious of these. The majority of saddlery is made of leather. Apart from its pleasing appearance, it is the best material for the job. Strong, durable, it does not rot easily, will not fray, and can 'breathe'. It is also comfortable for both the horse and rider, and yields well to the demands made of it, such as being stretched over the seat of the saddle. Since it is natural, it is unlikely to cause skin reactions or allergies, unless it has been badly cared for.

Other commonly-used natural fibres are *cotton and flax webbs.* Examples of the uses of cotton webb are in lunge reins, girths and reins; it is strong, kind to the rider's hands and to the horse. Its big disadvantage lies in the fact that it does rot in contact with wet and sweat, so needs care and observation. Flax webb is most frequently used as attachments for the girth straps – as it is already pre-stretched it does not give easily, and so is ideally suited to this purpose.

Cotton and wool union webb is used for items such as girths, overgirths, surcingles, and breast girths. Another natural fibre, it is stronger than cotton webb, but the disadvantage once again is that it rots. All webb, of whatever type, needs to be checked regularly for signs of rotting, and also signs of wearing and fraying, especially where it comes into contact with metal fittings.

Nowadays there are many proprietary brands of rugs. Traditional materials for these are natural: *wool* for day rugs, *jute* for night rugs, *canvas* with woollen linings for New Zealand rugs.

Kersey and *Boxcloth* are most commonly used for boots – either as the finished article or as a lining. These natural, hardwearing woollen materials are useful in that, kept clean, they do not rub or irritate the skin.

The last of these natural fibres is *flock* with which saddles and rollers are stuffed. Ideally it should be of pure white wool, although more often it is woollen waste which has been teased out; but this is still better than the acrylic or carpet waste found in cheaper saddles.

Moving onto synthetic materials, which are more frequently seen now, one of the most popular is *nylon webb* used for girth strap webbs, headcollars and such like. Its popularity owes much to the fact that it is extremely strong, easily cared for, and very resistant to rotting. However, a check should be kept on it during routine maintenance, as poor quality nylon frays very easily. Nylon webb is increasing in popularity for use in exercise bridles, since it is easy and cheap. A major problem is that its great strength could lead to an accident should a horse or pony become entangled for some reason. Leather will eventually break when placed under strain and so is less likely to injure the animal.

Vinyl and *plastic* are seen more often now than in the past, since they keep the cost of producing saddlery to a minimum. They will not absorb water, are easily washed, and will not rot as natural fibres do, but if used directly against the horse's skin, will make it sweat. They also become brittle over the years and disintegrate, making replacement necessary.

'Furniture' – as the metal fittings (excluding bits) on saddlery are referred to – should always be inspected when considering purchase. *Stainless steel* is popular, although expensive. It has an attractive grey sheen, does not rust, is strong and usually has a good finish. *Solid nickel* has similar properties; it does not rust, is strong, although not as much so as stainless steel, and is recognisable by its off-white colour, which requires more effort in keeping it shiny. It is suitable, and very commonly used for buckles since it is cheaper than steel, but is not ideal for bits and stirrup irons as it can bend and snap if placed under great strain.

Stirrup bars on saddles are sometimes cast, but for safety should be of *forged steel* and stamped to that effect.

Nickel plate is also fairly strong, but the plating quickly wears off, and it becomes rusty. *Cadmium plating* is a heavy plating designed to withstand the rigours of weather and outdoor activities, and can be identified by its dull white finish. It is frequently seen on furniture for New Zealand rugs (buckles and clips) and also on headcollar clips. *Brass* is an attractive, shiny yellow colour, which requires a certain amount of polishing to maintain its appearance. It is reasonably strong, but the tongues of brass buckles should be made of steel as brass will bend too easily. The tongues are sprayed gold to match the rest of the buckle, although this soon wears off with use. In Indian saddlery the tongues are often made of brass as well, which could prove dangerous. Some makes of saddle also have stirrup bars made of brass.

Saddle trees – the framework around which the leather is attached – are generally constructed from beechwood. Obviously this is prone to damage if dropped or badly stored, so care should be taken.

Identifying good quality saddlery

The prospective purchaser should look first at the quality of the leather rather than the colour. It should feel firm and greasy, yet supple and pliable. It should also be suitable for the job it is required to do; thinner and lighter for a show bridle, or coarser and with more substance for roller and headcollar. The different colours depend upon the factory the leather comes from, as all have their own dyes and names. The most common are 'London' which is a tan colour, 'Havana', a red brown colour, and 'Warwick', a dark nut tone. 'Chrome' leather is white in colour and has been processed to make it more water-resistant. It is able to take a greater amount of strain, making it ideal for leg straps on New Zealand rugs, and is often seen on girth straps on saddles. In the case of the latter it tends to stretch too much.

Inspect the quality of the furniture used, as good quality work should not have cheap, unsafe fittings. Similarly, cheap workmanship will probably not exhibit expensive, quality furniture.

Next, the stitching should be closely looked at, the most important point being that it should be neat, showing that care has been taken in its production and finishing. The stitches should be quite small, the number being dependent upon the piece. For quality bridlework, it should be possible to count between 10–12 stitches to the inch; 8 stitches to the inch for stirrup leathers, girths, headcollars and heavier work, and about 7 stitches to the inch for rugs.

The thread used should be either *linen* or *nylon*. Nylon is strong and does not rot easily, but is not always ideal as it can fray and become unstitched; it also tends to pull through leather. Linen rots quite easily, but is strong and suited to its purpose, provided checks are regularly made on it. *Cotton* thread is frequently seen in Indian saddlery, and since it rots extremely quickly, is not particularly safe. All threads are waxed with *beeswax* if the saddlery has been handstitched, which helps to preserve the thread against the weather.

Best bridlework is stitched up with a double handed stitch, so that when looking at it, it appears to be the same on both sides. Backstitch looks like one long stitch on the reverse side, is not so tight, is more likely to rub the horse, and will wear out more quickly too. A lot of factory made goods are produced like this as it is easy for an inexperienced worker to produce relatively competently. However, where leather is sewn to material, as in boots and rugs for example, backstitch should be used as it prevents the thread from being pulled right through the material.

Maintenance

Even good quality saddlery will rapidly deteriorate if it is not properly looked after and nourished.

Leather will suffer from damp storage conditions, or by being exposed constantly to heat or sunlight, so it should be kept somewhere dry and cool. Ideally it should be cleaned each time it is used.

To clean leather items of saddlery thoroughly, they should be taken apart, or 'stripped down' completely. When undoing hook studs, care must be taken not to place stress on the keepers, which can easily break. Firstly, all dirt, sweat, and grease should be removed by washing with a sponge or cloth and hot water with a little detergent added to it. It is important that all of the dirt is removed completely before nourishing, as the pores in the leather will otherwise become clogged up. Then, despite having an attractive appearance, and perhaps feeling quite supple, the leather dries out in the centre and is likely to snap with little or no warning. This is one of the hazards of buying second-hand saddlery, since it is impossible to tell how well it has really been cared for in the past. Avoid making the leather too wet, as this will damage it as much as not cleaning it at all; it will be too waterlogged to absorb any dressing.

Each time saddlery is used, the leather loses some of its fat content because the heat and sweat of the horse dries it out. This fat should be replaced, by using a leather dressing of some kind – either a bar of glycerine soap, or one of the proprietary brands available. This should be thoroughly worked into the leather on both sides. If the saddlery has become soaked, remove the dirt, and then allow it to dry out naturally, but nourish it once or twice during the process. After this it can then be given an application of neatsfoot oil. New leather should also be oiled frequently in order to make it more supple and comfortable for the horse; probably about ten times in all. The tack should be cleaned first, and the oil used instead of saddle soap once a week.

Metal buckles and furniture should be washed, and a metal polish can be used if desired. However, polish should not be used on the mouthpieces of bits, nor should it be allowed to come into contact with any leather. A bunch of horsehair is a useful alternative to metal polish if rubbed vigorously against the metal, and curb chains can be kept bright by placing them in a small bag of bran, and carrying them around in a pocket for a while.

Nylon headcollars, girths, and so on, are easily washable in hot soapy water, and should be well rinsed so that the detergent causes no skin irritations. Cotton, linen and lampwick can be similarly washed, but any leather attached must be oiled or vaselined first to protect it from drying and cracking, and oiled yet again when the article is dry.

Tack should be properly stored if left unused for long periods of time. A thorough cleaning is necessary first, preferably using a strong solution of Milton sterilising fluid to destroy any mould in the leather. Next, a covering of Ko-cho-line will ensure that the leather does not become dry or brittle. It should be kept in dry, cool conditions, and preferably covered with a sheet or proper cover to keep dust off. Saddles must be left on a proper rack or stand to avoid any damage, whilst bridles should be hung on a rounded peg so that the head piece keeps its shape.

Rugs and other material items of clothing are best kept cleaned and stored with mothballs in a large trunk or case set aside for the purpose.

2

BUYING SADDLERY

Buying saddlery is expensive especially when kitting out a horse completely. A complete set of equipment can actually cost more than the price of the animal it is intended for! However, it is best in the long run not to buy cheap and inferior saddlery. Good quality materials and workmanship will not only last longer, but be safer, and less expensive in terms of major repairs.

When buying tack for the first time, the best approach is usually to ask a reputable local saddler to travel over with a selection of saddles to try out. Finding a saddle which fits both horse and rider correctly is hardly ever straightforward, and this tactic does cut down on time spent travelling back and forth with one saddle on each trip. There is also the bonus of having advice on the fit of a particular saddle from somebody experienced in the subject.

Buy the 'essentials', and add extra pieces at a later date. A stable kept, or partially stabled animal is likely to require more equipment than its grass kept alternative; but whether saddlery and equipment is bought new or secondhand, the very best quality should be sought. The better the quality, the longer its life expectancy, and the less depreciation should it be resold at a future date – provided of course that it is looked after properly.

Often the problem for the new owner is to establish exactly what is necessary, and what can be left out. Buying saddlery sold with a horse or pony is not always the best idea; often it is a set of inferior tack thrown together in order to boost the price of the animal, although sometimes perfectly genuine tack is offered.

Suggested below are items which will need to be bought for animals in both stabled and grass kept conditions.

Stable kept

Bridle (plus martingale if needed)
General purpose saddle and buckle guards
Girth
Stirrup irons
Stirrup leathers
Bit
Headcollar and lead rope/hemp halter
Jute or stable rug
Roller/surcingle
Sweat sheet
Mucking out tools – wheelbarrow, pitchfork, broom, shovel and skip
Tack cleaning equipment – soap, oil, sponges, metal polish
Grooming kit
First aid kit
New Zealand rug if turned out at all during the winter

Optional

Numnah/saddlecloth
Blankets
Fillet string
Day rug and matching surcingle/roller
Summer sheet and matching surcingle/roller

Grass kept

Bridle (and martingale if needed)
Saddle and buckle guards

Girth
Stirrup irons
Stirrup leathers
Bit
Headcollar and lead rope/hemp halter
New Zealand rug
Grooming kit
Tack cleaning equipment
First aid kit
Fly fringe or repellent

Optional
Numnah/saddlecloth

We suggest the grooming kit is made up from the following articles: dandy brush, body brush, stable rubber, plastic/rubber curry comb, metal/rubber curry comb, hoof oil and brush, hoofpick, sponges for nostrils, eyes and dock, tail bandage, mane and tail comb, trimming scissors.

The first aid kit should include the following: veterinary thermometer, Vaseline, fly repellent, antiseptic cream, wound powder, gamgee, cotton wool, salt, four stable bandages, two crêpe bandages, scissors.

Buying secondhand tack is the option that faces many horse owners, unable to afford the cost of the much preferable new equipment. But there are many pitfalls for the inexperienced in such matters. Auctions of tack are best avoided, as much is either badly damaged, or of poor quality. It is usually difficult to pick up a genuine 'bargain' at such sales.

Secondhand saddlery is best bought from a source where it will be possible to exchange unsuitable items – a local saddler for example, may well have a selection of secondhand goods available as well as new. Check first the possibilities of exchange or refunds. Care must be exercised in the inspection of secondhand saddlery, as no saddler will take back a saddle with a broken tree, for example, if the damage could easily have been the fault of the purchaser. Where major repairs are necessary, buying secondhand will not be economic, and so an experienced friend's advice should be sought.

Leather
The leather on saddlery, especially that bought secondhand, should be firm and greasy. This is an indication that it is in good condition, or has been well cared for in the past. It should be pleasantly supple and the right sort of thickness for the job it is required for. A headcollar ought to be made of more substantial leather, while a bridle should be finer, and of a better quality of leather. The surface should not be dry, or appear blistered or wrinkled. In secondhand saddlery, weak points should be very carefully looked for, particularly any places where the leather is likely to become worn; at attachments to the bit, holes which have run together, and so forth. Reins and stirrup leathers should not be purchased if they have broken and been repaired, other than restitching at the buckles or hook studs. They have to take a great deal of strain, and the rider's safety depends upon them. A repair to a break means a potentially weak point.

Stitching
Tug gently at any stitching to check that it is safe. Overlarge stitches are an indication of cheap saddlery; the appropriate number of stitches to the inch should be used for the particular item (see page 14). Bridlework which has been backstitched will also wear very quickly, and probably rub.

Furniture
'Furniture' or the metal fittings on saddlery, are a fairly good

guide as to the quality of a piece. The better the quality of the furniture, the better the quality of the leather is likely to be. Fittings should be in good condition, and, if secondhand, not suffering from the effects of age – the tongues on the buckles should still be long enough, not worn so short that they are likely to be pulled through to the back.

Buckles and hook studs have a tendency to snap on Indian saddlery, and the tongues of the buckles to bend. Indian products should be avoided where possible, as although the standard of workmanship has improved over the last few years, the quality of the materials used has not, and is usually substandard. They frequently have distinctive rounded buckles, and any brass buckles used often have a matching brass tongue too, which is likely to bend when put under stress. On quality work, the brass buckles will have a steel tongue instead, which is much stronger. Although it is sprayed gold when new, so that it matches the rest of the buckle, with time the colouring wears off, and in second-hand saddlery, is visible.

Indian tack can also be identified by the unpleasant pungent smell of the leather if it is still fairly new, plus a distinctive yellowish colouring. It feels unpleasant to touch, and is often heavily grained in addition. Older saddles will be a slightly odd shape, and perhaps quilted underneath as well.

Saddles

It is much easier to pick out potential safety hazards in bridles and headcollars than it is in saddles. The first and probably most important point to check on is that the 'tree', forming the framework around which the saddle is built, is still intact. A broken tree will be expensive to repair, even to the extent that it might prove cheaper to buy a new saddle. A saddle with a broken tree cannot be used without attention, since it will cause discomfort and sores on the horse's back. Even if the expense of repair is undertaken, the future life expectancy cannot be guaranteed; the repair could last several years, one year, or less. See fig 1, page 23.

The most common places for a break to occur are either across the front arch, or across the waist of the saddle, but it is possible to check for weaknesses in these places. The saddle should first be placed on a table, or flat surface, so that the front is facing you. Place the heel of each palm on each point, and press them firmly towards each other; movement or squeaking will indicate a break across the front arch. Next, the saddle should be held so that the cantle, or back of the saddle rests against the breastbone. Hold the front arch firmly with both hands, and pull it towards the breastbone; movement will indicate a break across the waist of the tree, or weak springs.

Other signs that might suggest a break somewhere in the tree are that the saddle will probably creak when in use, and a crease may be visible in the leather stretched across the seat. Testing a saddle for soundness does require a certain amount of experience if a correct judgment is to be made of its condition, so several other saddles should be examined similarly at the same time in order to compare the amount of movement.

The majority of saddles nowadays are 'spring trees' rather than the old 'rigid' variety, so as to be more comfortable for the rider. The name refers simply to two long pieces of curved metal stretching along the length of the saddle; but a big disadvantage is that the increased flexibility makes an accurate diagnosis of the condition of the tree difficult without actually taking the saddle apart – hence the need for a certain amount of experience. After the age of about five years, some 'spring trees' are also prone to distortion and twisting, causing pain and sores on the horse's back, so that any secondhand saddle with a great deal of movement is best discarded.

Excessive wear on the flaps, seat and panels should be

taken into account, as damage to these areas is difficult as well as costly to repair, and will make the saddle rather unsightly. Whether new or secondhand, saddles which have a great deal of additional stitching on the flaps or panels are likely to cause future problems, in that the stitching will inevitably wear very quickly, being in a place where friction and sweat will affect it, so that frequent repairs will be necessary. Hide covered saddles also tend to wear badly.

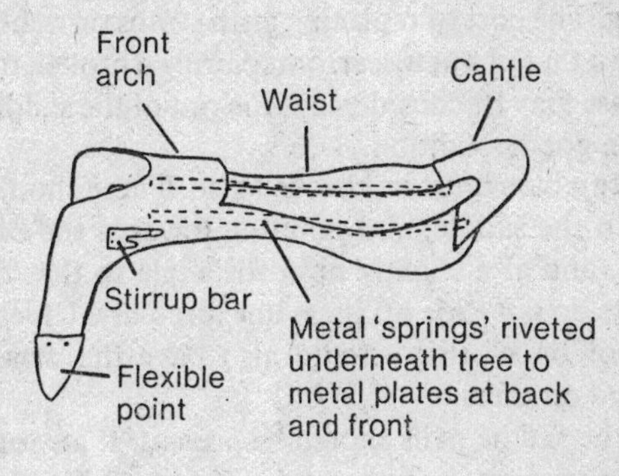

1 (*Above*) A saddle tree.

(*Below*) There should be three girth straps on each side.

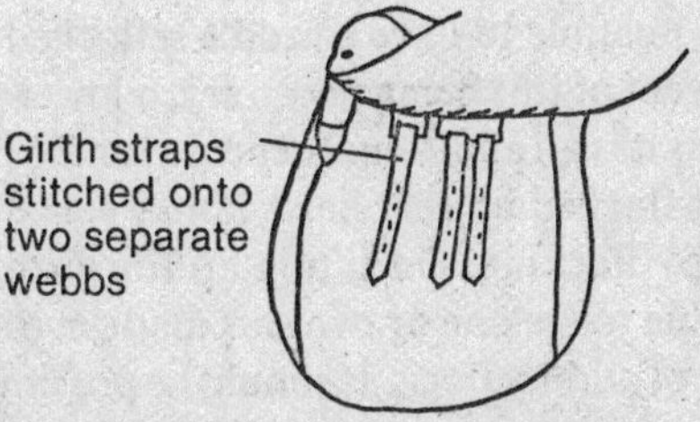

Girth straps
stitched onto
two separate
webbs

A careful examination of the girth straps is important, if the saddle, complete with rider, is not to part company with the horse. There should be three girth straps on each side of the saddle (see fig 1), in good repair, and with two of the three straps attached to a separate piece of webbing from the third. This is a safety precaution, so that in the event of one webb breaking, the second will take the strain and prevent a disaster from occurring. The webbing should also be in good repair – a close scrutiny should not reveal any signs of fraying. The cost of replacing girth straps or webbs is much less than that of a new seat, or repairing a broken tree, and so purchase may be considered if the rest of the saddle appears to be in good condition.

Stirrup bars must be checked also. These should be lying close to the saddle, and pointing towards the back of the saddle, and at a slightly upwards angle so that the stirrup leathers do not slide off them unexpectedly. Unless they are made of brass, they should also have the word 'forged' stamped on them.

All the saddle nails should be present. If any of these are loose or missing altogether, there is a possibility that the tree is in bad condition, and probably rather suspect.

The underside of the saddle should be as closely inspected as the top parts. Both panels should be as equal in size as possible so as not to cause uneven weight distribution on the back muscles. The flock, or stuffing, inside should not feel lumpy. It is possible to have a saddle reflocked completely, but in the event of this being necessary, a lower price should be offered, as it is an additional expense for the purchaser. If the saddle is flocked up very hard, it may cause a sore back, as will lumpy flocking. On lifting up the girth straps, you should be able to see one or two slits made in the leather for the purpose of adding flock. It should be possible to pull out a small amount, which should consist of a woollen mixture of white, brown, or a greyish colour. Cheaper saddles are filled with something which resembles multicoloured carpet waste. This can also be an indication of an Indian saddle, using cheaper materials.

When buying a new or secondhand saddle, it is advisable to buy one which either fits exactly when not flocked up over hard, or which is slightly on the narrow side (provided that it is not so narrow that it pinches) because it will stretch to a degree if used on a broader horse than it was originally intended for. But a saddle which is too wide and needs plenty of flocking to make it fit is going to need continual adjustment to make it sit comfortably.

Saddles are usually described in inch sizes. The number of inches – most commonly 14", 15", 16", 17", and 18", refers to the distance between the nails on the pommel to the centre of the cantle, in a straight line. The size of the seat should be appropriate for the size of the rider, although the underneath of the saddle must fit the horse or pony concerned. The type of saddle should also be suitable for the job – a jumping saddle would be inappropriate for use in dressage, for example.

Rugs

Rugs can be bought new at fairly reasonable prices, since they are easier to mass-produce than saddles or bridles, so it is usually better to buy new rather than secondhand, unless the rug is in very good condition. They are bought in various lengths, from 4′6" and upwards to 6′6" long, in 3" distances. They are more commonly measured from the chest to the back of the rug, and it is this measurement – not from the withers to the back of the rug – which should be taken when deciding upon the correct size.

Disinfection

Any saddlery or horse clothing bought secondhand should always be disinfected to avoid the danger of skin diseases being passed on. It is also possible for skin infections to start up if the tack has been allowed to go mouldy at sometime in the past, even if it has been thoroughly cleaned since that time. Everything should be washed with a strong solution of Milton sterilising fluid, which will not irritate the skin, or damage leather and other materials, as harder disinfectants may do.

3

BRIDLES

Bridles generally belong to one of five main groups: the snaffle bridle, double bridle, gag snaffle, Pelham bridle, and bitless bridle.

Snaffle bridle

A snaffle bridle consists of:

headpiece with throatlash
browband
two cheekpieces
noseband (see NOSEBANDS, Chapter 5)
snaffle bit (see BITS, Chapter 4)
one pair of reins (see REINS, Chapter 6)

The bit of a snaffle bridle places pressure upon the bars of the mouth (see fig 9, page 40), tongue, corners of the mouth, and via the cheekpieces and headpiece of the bridle, to a very small degree, upon the poll.

The browband may be plain, fancy stitched for showing purposes, of raised leather, or decorated with brass, leather plaiting, or similar. Browbands used in showing classes are often covered with velvet to match the rider's turnout.

The cheekpieces may be stitched to the bit to give a neater appearance in showing classes, or alternatively attached by means of hook studs (see fig 3), which makes routine cleaning and repairs easier.

2 Parts of a snaffle bridle

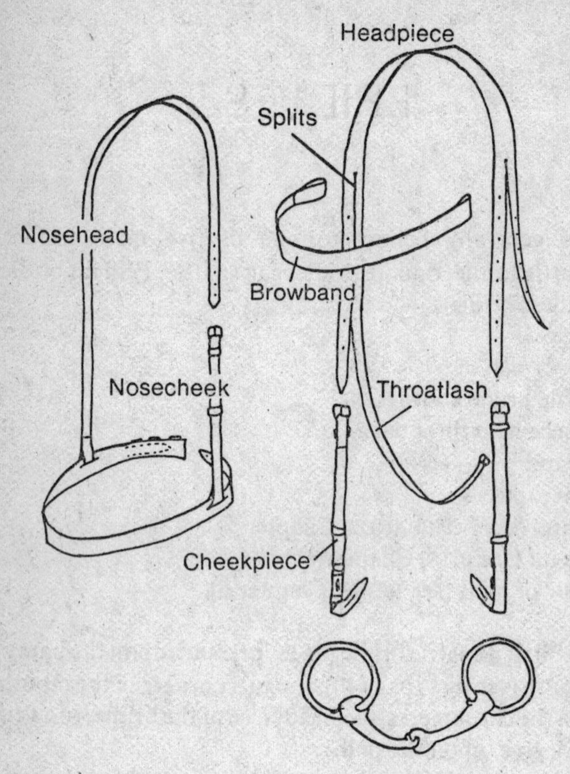

3 Hook stud

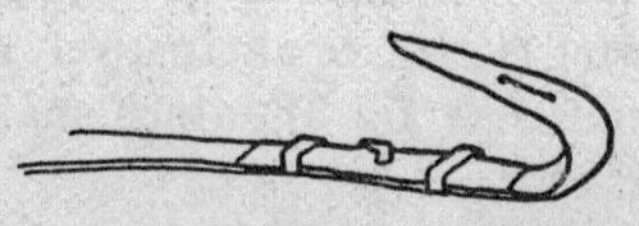

Fitting

The headpiece must be sufficiently long so that when the browband is in place and the throatlash fastened, the splits at either side do not divide and push the browband up into the base of the ears, causing discomfort. Ideally, the splits should terminate just beneath the browband, as shown in fig 4.

4 Fitting a snaffle bridle

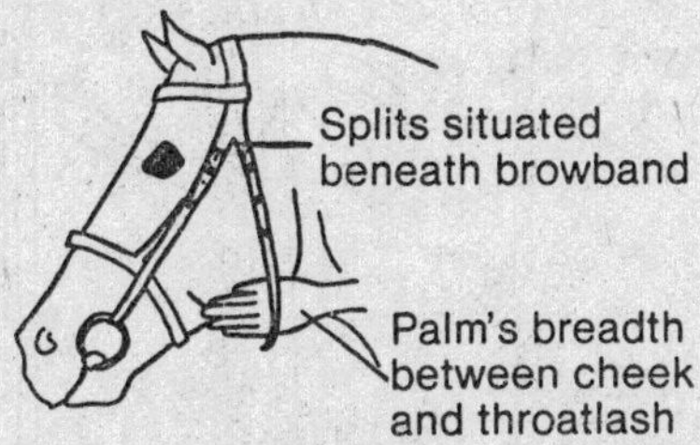

The browband itself ought not to be so long that it drops downwards, and allows the headpiece to slide back, but more importantly, it should not be so short that it pulls the headpiece forward into the ears.

Once properly adjusted, there should be room for a palm's breadth (approximately 4") between the throatlash and the throat, as shown in fig 4. If it is any looser than this it will not perform its function of preventing the bridle from slipping off over the horse's ears in an emergency, whilst any tighter than this will restrict the breathing when the animal tries to work correctly.

The cheekpieces, when adjusted so that the bit is lying at the proper height in the mouth, should be done up on a hole which is approximately halfway up the number provided on the headpiece. This then leaves plenty of room for further adjustment to be made if the bridle stretches, is required for use on another horse, or in the event of breakages. The cheekpieces should be done up at the same height on both sides to ensure that the bit lies evenly in the mouth.

The bit itself should lie high enough in the mouth just to wrinkle the corners of the lips. An easy way of checking the fitting is gently to take up a contact on both reins; if all is as it

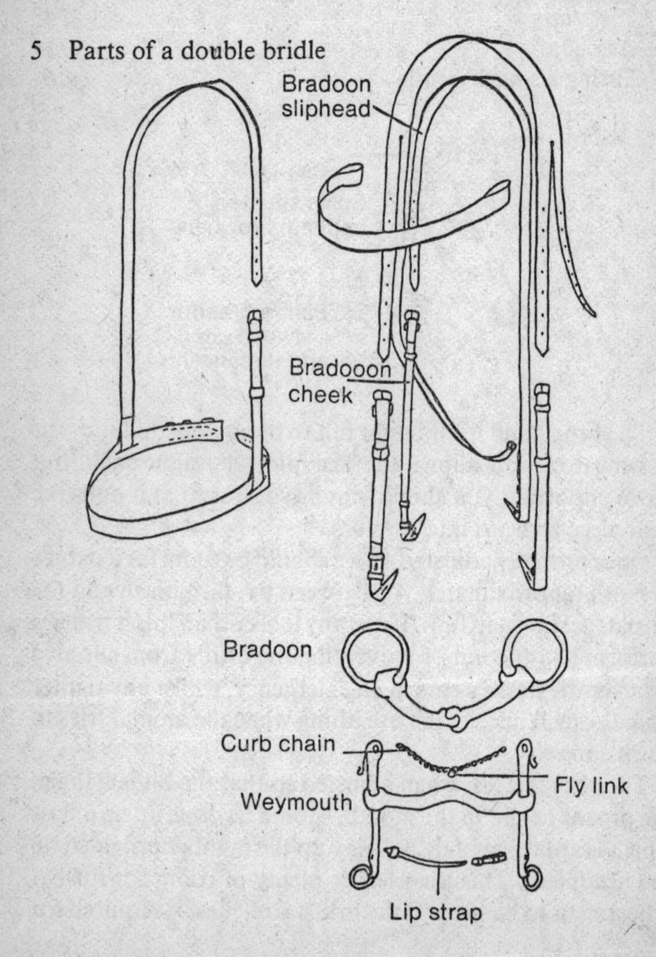

5 Parts of a double bridle

should be, then the cheekpieces will not 'bag' outwards and become slack.

The noseband headpiece should be threaded through the loops at either end of the browband, and lie beneath the bridle headpiece.

Double bridle

A double bridle is made up of:

headpiece with throatlash
browband
two cheekpieces } see SNAFFLE BRIDLE, page 27
cavesson noseband (see NOSEBANDS, Chapter 5)
bradoon sliphead plus cheekpiece
curb chain (see ACCESSORIES TO THE BRIDLE, Chapter 9)
lip strap (see ACCESSORIES TO THE BRIDLE, Chapter 9)
two pairs of reins (see REINS, Chapter 6)
Weymouth
bradoon } (see BITS, Chapter 4)

The double bridle is intended for use in more advanced schooling, so that in conjunction with the rider's leg, back and seat aids, it can produce a greater degree of flexion and collection. A double bridle is also frequently required in show classes for correct turnout, but should not be used until the horse will accept an ordinary snaffle bit properly. The two bits act, in conjunction with the bridle, on the poll, bars of the mouth, tongue, chin groove and the corners of the mouth. The bradoon and Weymouth bits are normally bought as a set, but the bradoon should be ¼" longer than the Weymouth, since it sits higher, and consequently in a broader part of the jaw. To help the rider differentiate between the two reins without continually having to look down, the Weymouth rein should be slightly narrower than the bradoon. See fig 5.

Fitting

The bridle is assembled similarly to the snaffle bridle, except that the Weymouth, or curb bit, is attached to the cheekpieces which normally take the snaffle bit. The bradoon, or snaffle bit, is fastened to the bradoon sliphead and cheekpiece, which should lie so that the buckle is to the off side, so that there are only two buckles on either side of the face. Together with the noseband headpiece, it should slot through the loops in each end of the browband.

Fitting a double bridle is the same as for a snaffle bridle as regards the length of browband, throatlash, and so forth. The height of the bits are slightly different, however. The bradoon should be fitted a little higher than an ordinary snaffle, with the Weymouth lying lower than this, leaving a gap of approximately ¼″ between the mouthpieces of each bit at the point where they are visible at the corners of the mouth.

When putting the double bridle on, both bits should be offered to the horse at the same time. If they are adjusted at the correct heights, the horse will settle them in the right place in its mouth, regardless of whether the bradoon lay on top of or underneath the Weymouth when it was offered.

The curb chain should be twisted so that it lies flat in the chin groove, passing between bradoon and Weymouth. It should not be too tight, but come into contact with the chin groove when the shanks of the Weymouth are drawn back at an angle of 45° to the mouth. In the centre of the curb chain is an extra link (fly link) through which the lip strap should be threaded. The lip strap can be fastened so that it remains fairly slack, and does not interfere with the action of the curb chain.

Gag snaffle

This bridle consists of:

headpiece with throatlash } see SNAFFLE BRIDLE, (page 27)
browband }
noseband (see NOSEBANDS, Chapter 5)
two pairs of reins (see REINS, Chapter 6)
gag snaffle bit (see BITS, Chapter 4)
two sliding cheekpieces

6 A gag snaffle

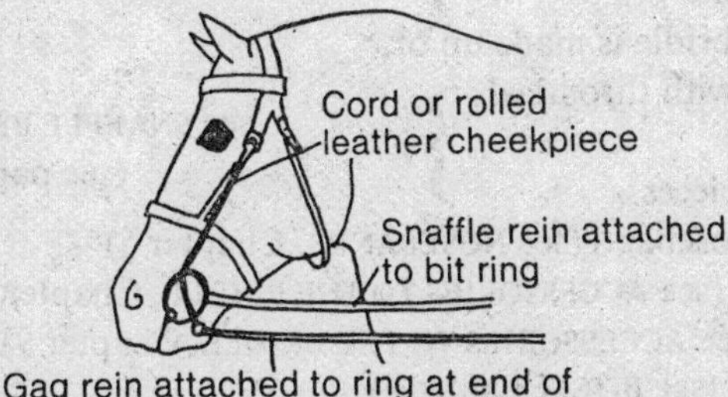

This type of bridle has a very strong raising action when the gag rein is employed, and a similar effect to that of an ordinary snaffle when the snaffle rein only is used. It also places an increased pressure on the poll.

The cheekpieces differ from those of other bridles in that they are made of either cord or rolled leather. This allows them to slide freely through two holes, one in the top, and one in the bottom, of each bit ring. Two reins are required in order to allow the rider to use the bridle as either a gag, or an ordinary snaffle, as shown in fig 6.

The gag rein, used to raise the head of a horse which bears down strongly on the bit, should not be continually engaged, otherwise the horse will become accustomed and eventually hardened against its action, and the effect will be lost.

Fitting

The bridle should be fitted in the same way as an ordinary snaffle bridle. The bit, when resting at the fullest extent of the rolled cheekpiece, should be at the same height as a normal snaffle bit. One pair of reins is attached to the bit as normal, the other pair to the rolled cheekpieces where they pass through the bottom of the bit rings.

Pelham bridle

A Pelham bridle is made up of:
headpiece with throatlash, browband, two cheekpieces } see SNAFFLE BRIDLE (see page 27)
cavesson noseband (see NOSEBANDS, Chapter 5)
curb chain (see ACCESSORIES TO THE BRIDLE, Chapter 9)
lip strap (see ACCESSORIES TO THE BRIDLE, Chapter 9)
Pelham bit (see BITS, Chapter 4)
two pairs of reins, or roundings and one pair of reins (see REINS and ACCESSORIES TO THE BRIDLE)

The Pelham is intended to combine the principles behind the double bridle within one bit. It should really be used with two pairs of reins so that either a snaffle or curb action can be obtained, but is frequently used with just one pair of reins attached to leather roundings on the bit. This latter course of action is most usually adopted by novice riders who are unable to co-ordinate the two reins. A Pelham can be useful in situations where a horse or pony is likely to become very strong and perhaps ignore the action of a snaffle bit – when hunting or riding across country perhaps.

Fitting

The bridle should be fitted in the same way as the snaffle bridle, although the bit should be slightly lower if it is not of the jointed variety. Careful fitting of the curb chain is required, as otherwise there is a danger of its riding upwards out of the chin groove. It should come into contact with the jawbone when the shanks of the bit are drawn back at an angle of 45° to the mouth.

The reins are attached to the snaffle ring of the bit, and a second pair to the bottom ring on the shank of the bit. Alternatively, a rounding made of substantial rolled or flat leather and fastened with hook studs, may be attached to the same places, and then a single rein fastened to this rounding.

Bitless bridle

This bridle consists of:

headpiece with throatlash } see SNAFFLE BRIDLE
browband } (see page 27)
two cheekpieces }
one pair of reins (see REINS, Chapter 6)
bitless bridle noseband

The most common form of bitless bridle is the 'Blairs' pattern (see fig 7), made up of two adjustable pieces of leather and two curved metal shanks, attached to the basic snaffle bridle. The front and back of the noseband should be well padded with sheepskin to prevent any chafing. Another form of bitless bridle, which is much milder, consists of a padded noseband front which is attached to the cheekpieces. At either end of the noseband front are large rings through which a soft leather strap passes. The reins are attached to this sliding backstrap. This form of bitless bridle is known as the 'Scawbrig' (see fig 8).

7 'Blairs' pattern bitless bridle

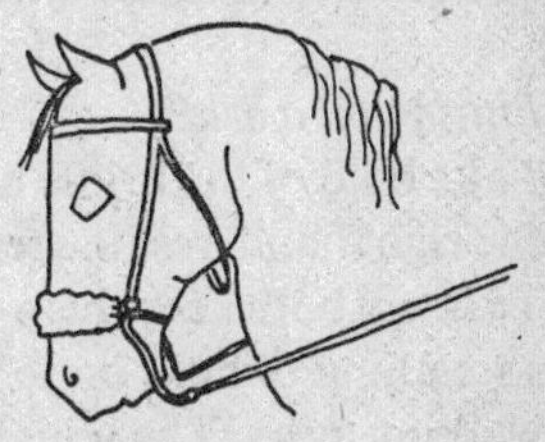

8 'Scawbrig' bitless bridle

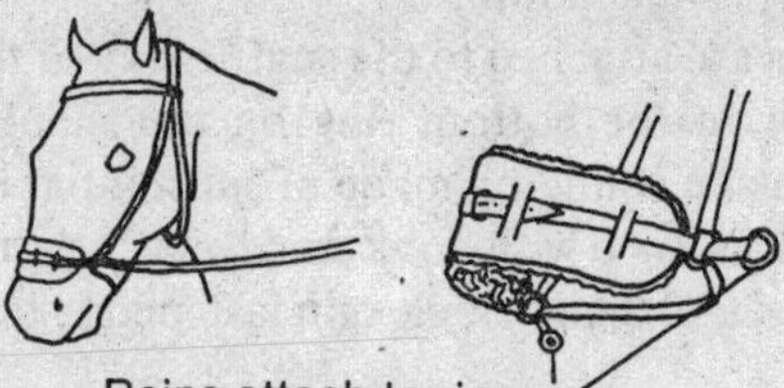

Reins attach to rings

The 'Blairs' pattern bitless bridle acts on the poll, nose, and back of the jaw. The longer the shanks, the more severe the action. It is useful in cases where for reasons of injury, or otherwise, a horse cannot be ridden in a bit. The second type of bitless bridle, the 'Scawbrig' is milder in its action, and exerts only a mild influence on the poll, pressure being directed mainly on the nose.

The height of both types of noseband should be regularly changed in order to prevent callouses.

Fitting

Both types of noseband should be fairly tightly fitted in order to be effective; hence the need for sufficient padding. They should be fitted well above the ending of the nasal cartilages, so as not to interfere with the breathing.

Putting on a bridle

Take hold of the bridle headpiece in the left hand, and with the right hand, rest the reins, doubled, over the horse's neck. This will both keep them out of the way, and give the handler something to hold on to in order to prevent the horse from walking away. The reins should not be actually looped over the neck, as, should the horse make a really determined attempt to escape, it is not possible to release it from the bridle, and a nasty accident could ensue should it become tangled up.

Standing close to the horse's neck and facing forwards, the right arm should be placed under the animal's jaw, and the hand brought around towards the centre of the face. This hand takes the bridle by the centre of both cheekpieces. The bit or bits should then be offered on the palm of the left hand; if the horse will not open its mouth to take the bit(s) then a thumb inserted at the corner of the mouth where there are no teeth, and pressed firmly downwards on the tongue should do the trick. As the mouth opens, the right hand should be raised, so as to lift the bit or bits gently.

The headpiece should be pushed over the horse's ears with the left hand, the offside ear first, and then the forelock settled comfortably beneath the bridle headpiece, and over the browband. Fasten the throatlash and noseband. Next the curb chain, and then the lip strap can be attached, if either is present.

When fitting a bridle for the first time, the heights of the buckles can be approximated by holding the bridle along the length of the head, and the runners and keepers should be left undone, so that if a readjustment needs to be made, it is much easier to effect quickly.

4

BITS

The bit is the rider's means of communicating his wishes to the horse or pony he is riding, in conjunction with signals from the rest of his body. Bits are made in a variety of materials, the most popular being stainless steel, nickel and nickel plate, whilst other materials are used for particular purposes. Rubber may be used for a sensitive mouth, or copper incorporated into the mouthpiece of a bit to encourage a wetter mouth.

Jointed bits should lie sufficiently high in the mouth so as just to wrinkle the corners of the lips. Straight bar bits need to be adjusted so that they are slightly lower than this, if they are to rest correctly on the bars of the mouth, without causing any discomfort. Many people make the mistake of letting the bit rest too low in the mouth, whereas it is in fact kinder as well as safer to have it slightly too high than too low. One which is too low will bang the front teeth, and encourage the horse or pony to play with it so that, before long, evasions arise such as putting the tongue over the bit.

Another very commonly seen error is that of buying a bit on which the mouthpiece is either too wide, or over-large. Especially where jointed snaffles are concerned, one which is too wide will have a severe 'nutcracker' action on the sides of the mouth, causing pinching. The joint may also rise up into the roof of the mouth, causing considerable pain, and there will certainly be plenty of room for the horse or pony to draw its tongue back and over the bit if it so wishes.

Some horses do have small, or short mouths, and a narrower mouthpiece on the bit should accordingly be selected if he is to be comfortable and accept the bit and the rider's rein contact with it. Most bits can be bought in sizes which progress in quarter inch steps, so there is no reason to buy one which is the wrong size. When the bit is in the horse or pony's mouth, there should be just sufficient room to insert a thumb on one side, between mouth and bit ring. Jointed bits should be held straightened out when checking the size.

Bits with wide mouthpieces are generally thought of as being mild, since pressure is spread out over a larger area, whilst narrower mouthpieces are severer since the pressure is concentrated on a small area. This does not necessarily mean that it is a kindness to select a larger mouthpiece, because of the reasons mentioned above. Also, if a horse or pony is inclined to lean on the bit, or pull, a narrower mouthpiece will make it respect the contact more, whilst the broader type is likely to allow it to persist in the habit. As the rider uses a progressively stronger contact in order to maintain control, so the nerve endings in the bars of the mouth will eventually become deadened and numb.

Snaffle bit

One of the most popular bits is probably the snaffle, of which there are numerous varieties. The jointed snaffle is the most common, and is of either an eggbutt or wire ring type.

An eggbutt snaffle helps to reduce the likelihood of rubbing and soreness at the corners of the mouth, and is a more 'set' bit, which a horse or pony is more likely to hold quietly in its mouth. A wire ring snaffle is ideal for those animals which lean against, or pull on, an eggbutt, since there is more movement to prevent this happening to such an extent.

A jointed snaffle bit acts on the corners of the lips, the bars (the part of the gums between the front and back teeth on the lower jaw), the tongue, and to a very limited degree, on the poll. See fig 9.

9 Parts of the horse's face

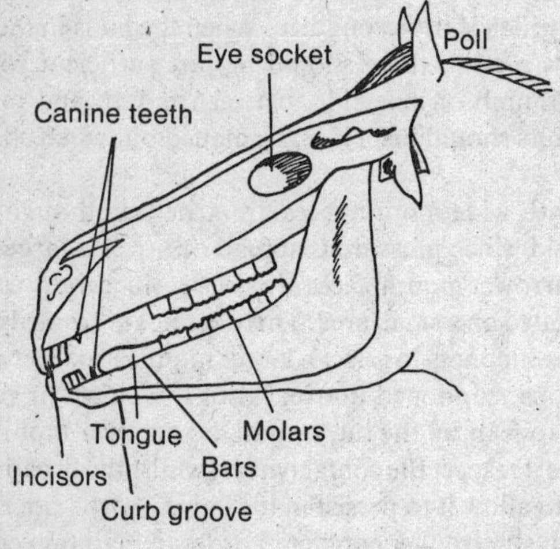

Some horses do not always work happily in a metal bit, and for these, a jointed snaffle which has been covered with rubber can be the answer. These usually have 'D' ring cheeks, in place of the normal rounded ones. A milder bit still is the straight bar snaffle, which may be manufactured from metal, or metal covered with rubber. The rubber is either vulcanised so that it is hard and inflexible, or it may be of plain rubber. Soft straight bar snaffles should have a chain inserted through the centre of the mouthpiece to minimise the danger of an accident should the rubber be severed. All these rubber and rubber covered bits tend to have large mouthpieces, and the straight bar variety, whether rubber or metal, can also make it difficult to achieve accurate steering.

Lacking a central joint, a straight bar snaffle is more difficult for a horse or pony to draw its tongue back over. The French link snaffle also has this advantage, whilst retaining the flexibility in the mouth of a jointed snaffle. It incorporates an extra joint into the mouthpiece, so that the squeezing 'nutcracker' action is lessened quite considerably. The extra joint encourages an animal to play with the bit and relax its jaw, but because it lies straighter in the mouth, it is difficult for the tongue to be displaced over it.

A bit often used on young horses is the Fulmer snaffle, which has long cheekpieces added to the mouthpiece. These help to encourage a novice animal to turn in the desired direction, whilst also making it impossible for the bit to be pulled through the mouth if it is opened in evasion. Fulmer keepers should be used with it to keep the cheekpieces in position.

More severe snaffles include the twisted snaffle and the Doctor Bristol. A Doctor Bristol bit can easily be confused with a French link, since it also has an extra joint in the mouthpiece. On closer inspection however, it will be seen that when held up, the Doctor Bristol link hangs at an angle so as to place additional pressure on the tongue and bars, whilst in the French link, the extra joint lies straight to the rest of the mouthpiece.

A twisted snaffle looks much as its name implies. The ridges along the mouthpiece make it much severer than a smooth bit.

Gag snaffle

This is a very powerful bit, used mainly on horses which tend to lean hard on to the rein contact, and which are difficult to stop. It has a very strong raising action on the head, due to the two sliding bridle cheekpieces which are threaded through the bit rings on either side. When the reins attached to these cheekpieces are employed, the bit is raised in the mouth and pressure exerted at the same time on the poll. It is best to use two pairs of reins, one set attached to the sliding cheekpieces, the other pair fastened as normal to the bit rings, so that the gag action is not continually in use. Otherwise the gag action would eventually deaden the mouth, so that it became less and less sensitive to the rider's wishes.

Double bridle

A double bridle has two bits, a snaffle and a curb, or a bradoon and a Weymouth as they should more correctly be called. The bradoon acts as a snaffle would do normally, whilst the Weymouth exerts an increased influence on the poll, bars of the mouth, and also on the curb groove. By use of these two bits a greater degree of collection can be obtained; but before being introduced to it, the horse or pony should first accept the contact of an ordinary snaffle bridle without fuss.

When fitting the bradoon and Weymouth, the bradoon should be adjusted slightly higher in the mouth than usual, so that the two bits do not interfere with one another's action. Buy a bradoon which is ¼" wider than the Weymouth, as it sits higher in the mouth, and therefore at a point where the jaw becomes wider. Some horses and ponies have very small mouths, and may find it difficult to cope with two bits if these are of the broader mouthpieced German type. In this case settle for narrower and lighter bits. The longer the shanks of the Weymouth, the more severe its action will be.

10 Various types of bit

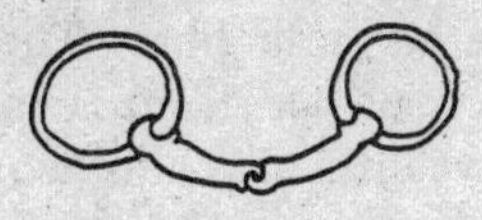

Wire ring snaffle

Fulmer

Straight bar snaffle

Twisted snaffle

French link

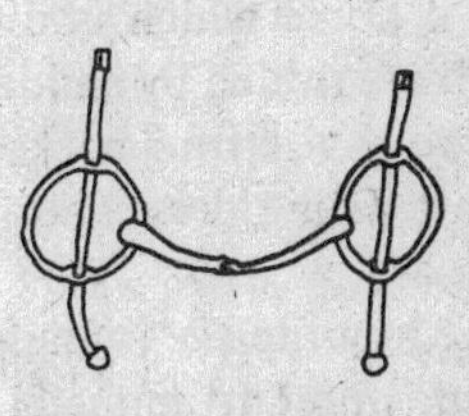

Gag snaffle

Pelham

Kimblewick

Pelhams and Kimblewicks

The Pelham bit is an attempt to combine the bradoon and Weymouth within one bit. It should really be used with two pairs of reins, although it is more frequently seen with one pair of reins attached to leather roundings. The latter method is much easier for a more novice rider to cope with, or a small child who might have difficulty with two sets of reins. Although a strong horse or pony can be satisfactorily controlled, it also follows that the influence of the curb is almost continual, and may come to be ignored. It is best to keep a stronger bit for occasions which really require it, such as when riding at speed, or in exciting conditions, and to keep a milder one for the rest of the time, provided it is safe to do so.

Despite its intentions, this bit does not successfully replace the two bits of a double bridle, but can be useful when coping with a horse which is difficult to stop. Although ponies which are ridden by children ought to have better manners, they do have strong necks and shoulders with which to pull against their riders, and this is why a stronger bit can be necessary.

The mouthpiece is made of vulcanite rubber, or metal; if manufactured from metal, it may sometimes include a port in the mouthpiece. This is a small raised section in the centre, which allows room for the tongue beneath the bit, helping to stop it from being placed over the mouthpiece – and which enables the rest of the bit to sit more directly onto the bars of the mouth.

Care should be taken when fitting the curb chain, as it rarely seems to rest in the curb groove, but on the jawbone instead. This can be a source of great irritation to some animals, and can cause sores.

The Kimblewick is another useful bit for a strong horse or pony which does not respect an ordinary snaffle. It is made of metal, and has a port in the centre of the mouthpiece. The advantage of the Kimblewick is that it does not require either an additional set of reins or roundings, and that the curb chain hangs much better in the curb groove. On some Kimblewicks, there is a choice of positioning for the reins, so that a milder or stronger curb effect can be obtained to suit the individual. This bit does involve a constant pressure on the poll and curb groove, however.

Bits are a topic to which a whole book could be devoted. Since there is so much variety, only a selection of the more commonly-used ones are covered in this chapter. When choosing a bit, the simpler the better. If problems do arise, then the rider should first look to his own riding or horse's physical problems such as ulcers, or sharp teeth. Secondly the method of schooling should be considered, and lastly the bit itself (other than for checks for worn edges). No proverb is more true than that of every twenty bits made, one is for the horse's mouth, and the other nineteen for the rider's head!

5

NOSEBANDS

Nosebands may be used for decorative purposes, or in order to correct an evasion, according to the type used. However, any noseband which passes around the chin groove should not be used in conjunction with a curb chain, as this could negate the effect of the chain, or lead to pinching and soreness.

Cavesson noseband

This is made of plain or raised leather, or perhaps fancy stitched to match the browband on a bridle suitable for showing classes. The noseband headpiece is either slotted through the noseband, or else stitched directly to it.

It is mainly used for appearance, to give a finishing effect to the bridle itself. In instances where a curb chain is needed, this noseband should be used, since it will not interfere with the chain. When a standing martingale is required, it should only be attached to a noseband of this sort, or to the cavesson part of a flash noseband.

Fitting

The headpiece is threaded through the ends of the browband, and lies inside the bridle headpiece. The noseband itself is fastened inside the bridle cheekpieces, rather than over them, since otherwise it could interfere with the position of the bit and its correct action. The height of the noseband should be such that it lies about halfway between the cheekbone and the corners of the mouth. Sufficient room is needed to admit two fingers' breadth between the noseband and the front of the face. If a standing martingale is going to be attached to it, then it should be fastened a little more firmly than this, but not so as to restrict the breathing.

Dropped noseband

Two-spiked rings are present in this noseband at the points where the headpiece joins onto the noseband (see fig 11). These rings each have two spikes, which are stitched into the noseband headpiece and noseband front, and this ensures that whilst the backstrap is free to drop downwards, the front strap will not. Attention should be given to this part of the noseband if the stitching in the area becomes worn out, as, once the spike is freed from the noseband front, that part will move downwards and begin to restrict the breathing. Sometimes an additional strip of leather is sewn diagonally from the base of the headpiece to the noseband front in order to help prevent this from happening, or this arrangement may be used if a plain ring is used instead of a spiked one.

11 A dropped noseband which needs a two-spiked ring

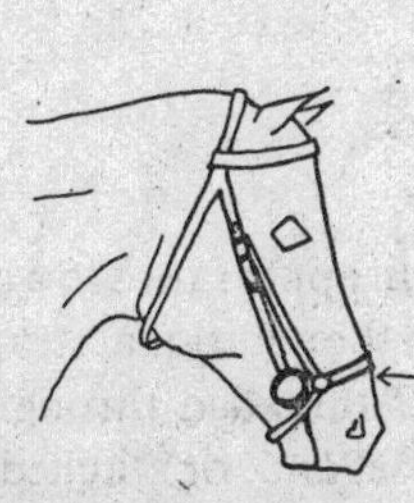

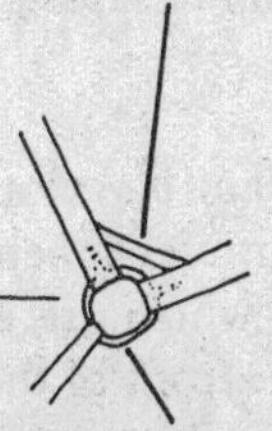

The aim of the noseband is to prevent evasion of the bit by the horse opening or crossing its jaws. If it tries to do either, pressure is placed on the front of the nose, which ceases when it relaxes again.

Fitting

The front of the noseband should lie approximately 3″ above the nostrils, although this measurement may vary slightly according to conformation. The rear strap should be long enough to drop below the bit so that it can sit comfortably in the chin groove without pushing the bit upwards in the mouth. The noseband front should not be too short, or else the cheekpieces will be pulled into the eyes. Conversely, should the noseband front be over-long, the back strap will not be positioned properly. The noseband needs to be fastened so that it prevents evasions, but not so tightly that it prevents flexion of the jaw, or interferes with breathing.

Sheepskin noseband

This is very similar to a cavesson noseband, excepting that the noseband front is covered with sheepskin.

It is commonly used as an 'anti-shying' device, or to prevent chafing. It is also supposed to be useful in cases where the horse stargazes, as it encourages it to lower its head in order to see ahead properly.

Fitting

As for a cavesson noseband.

Flash noseband

The flash noseband is very alike in appearance to a cavesson noseband, the difference being in the additional strap, or two crossing straps which are either threaded through a loop stitched into the front of the noseband, or stitched directly into place. See fig 12.

12 A flash noseband

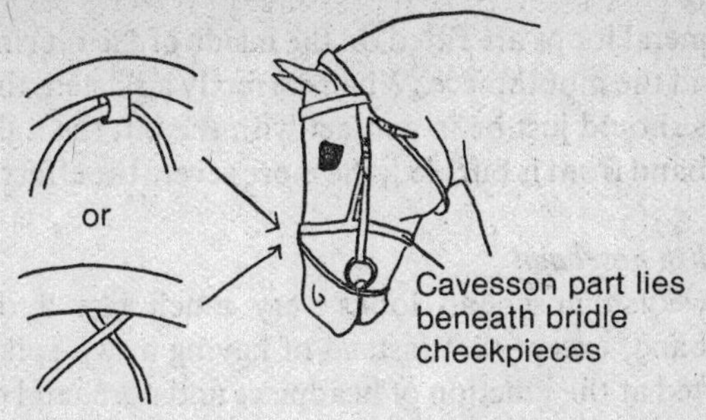

It is intended to have the same effect as a dropped noseband, although the pressure point on the nose, when the horse tries to evade, is rather higher. It is used in cases where a standing martingale as well as a dropped noseband are considered necessary; a standing martingale should never be used with a normal dropped noseband.

Fitting

The noseband is fitted at the same height as for a cavesson noseband, but sufficiently tightly to prevent the cavesson part dropping downwards when the additional strap or straps are buckled up. The cavesson part fastens inside the bridle cheekpieces. The dropped part lies beneath the bit. The standing martingale, if used, should be attached to the uppermost cavesson part of the noseband.

Kineton or Puckle noseband

The Kineton or Puckle noseband is used for horses which pull unduly; it places pressure on the nose when the horse tries to pull against the bit.

The noseband headpiece has a metal loop on either side, with an adjustable connecting nosepiece. It does not aim at actually closing the mouth in order to establish a greater amount of control over the horse.

Fitting

The metal loops are fitted on the inside of the bit rings, and behind the mouthpiece. When correctly adjusted, the metal loops should just be in contact with the bit; the tighter the noseband front is buckled, the more severe the effect will be.

Swedish noseband

A Swedish noseband looks very much like a dropped noseband, except that instead of having a two-spiked ring inserted at the junction of headpiece and noseband on both sides, a three-spiked ring is used. This prevents either the front or back of the noseband from dropping downwards. See fig 13.

13 A Swedish noseband

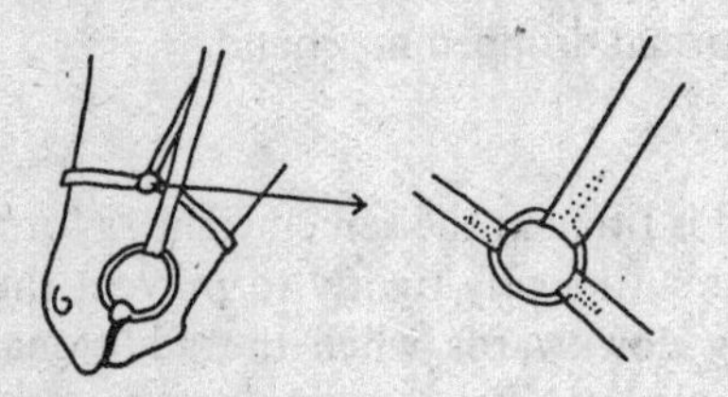

Three-spiked ring keeps noseband in position

Because pressure is exerted fairly high on the horse's nose, it will help to prevent bit evasions such as placing the tongue over the mouthpiece, or opening or crossing of the jaws.

Fitting

The noseband should be fitted at the same height as a cavesson, but much more tightly. There should be just sufficient room to admit one finger between the front of the noseband and the face.

Grakle noseband

This noseband concentrates pressure on the nose at the points where the two straps cross, so preventing the horse from opening its mouth, crossing its jaws, or putting its tongue over the bit in order to avoid the action.

It consists of a headpiece and two straps which cross one over the other in front of the face, and are fastened at the back of the jaw. The point at which they cross may be either fixed or movable, and should have some form of padding in the shape of a piece of sheepskin or soft leather. See fig 14.

14 A Grakle noseband

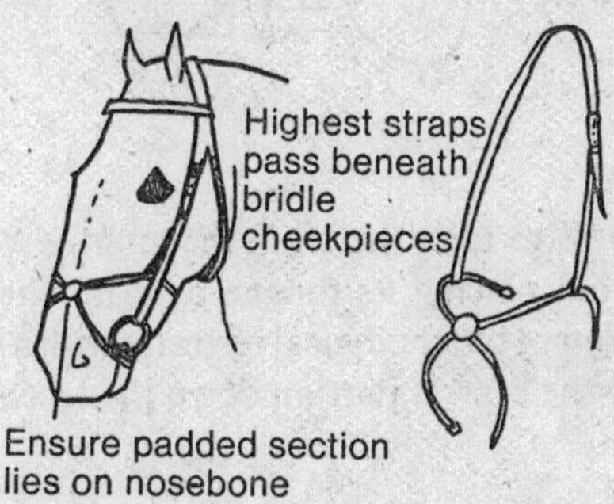

Fitting

Care must be taken that the noseband headpiece is not pulled forward at the sides into the horse's eyes. The uppermost straps pass beneath the bridle cheekpieces, whilst the lower ones drop beneath the bit, in the same manner as a dropped or flash noseband. They must be done up fairly tightly, so that just one finger can be admitted between the intersection of the two straps and the nosebone. It is important that the padded section rests on the nosebone and does not slip to one side over the nasal passages, which will impair breathing. The noseband headpiece should terminate on either side of the head at about two fingers' breadths below the cheekbones.

Australian cheeker

This is a strip of rubber which runs down the front of the face, where it divides into two, and is attached to the mouthpieces of the bit. See fig 15.

15 An Australian cheeker

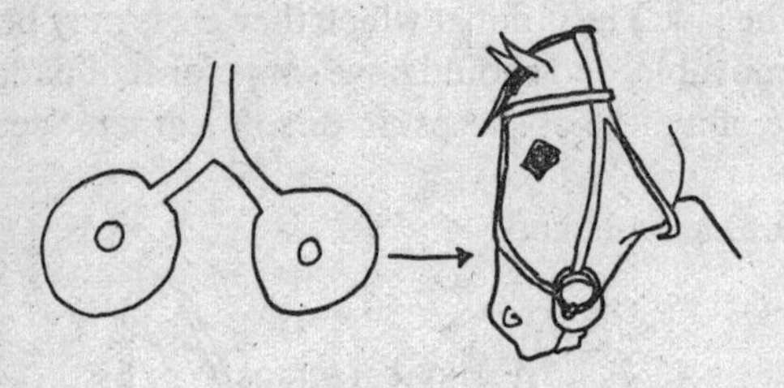

The object is to raise the bit in the mouth, so preventing the horse from placing its tongue over it. There is also a certain amount of psychological restraint with a horse which pulls, due to the central portion down the face.

Fitting

The top end should be attached to the centre of the bridle headpiece, between the ears. It then runs down the nosebone until it reaches a point at approximately the same height as a cavesson noseband would be fitted. Here it should divide, the rubber rings at the end of each division already being placed over the bit rings so that they lie between them and the lips. The noseband must, for obvious reasons, be fitted onto the bridle before placing it on the horse.

6

REINS

The reins are attached to the bit or noseband of the bridle. The wide variety of types available enables you to select a rein appropriate for any particular branch of riding. Reins also come in different widths, so care should be taken when buying; too wide a rein will be difficult for a small child to hold, whilst a very narrow rein will cut into the fingers of an adult. If reins are being purchased for a double bridle, or any bit where two pairs of reins are used, it is best to buy one narrow, one wider, pair of reins, so that it is easy to distinguish between the two without having to look down.

Plain leather

The reins may be attached to the bit either by hook studs, or by being stitched on. The latter method looks neater on a show bridle, but can lead to problems when cleaning and checking for signs of wear in a place which is under a great deal of strain. This area is also prone to become very dirty and covered in saliva, so good maintenance is essential. It also means that a spare bridle is necessary, in case repairs are needed, since the reins cannot be detached.

If two pairs of reins are being used, the wider rein is normally attached to the bradoon, and the thinner rein to the Weymouth, or to those parts of the bit which exert a similar action.

Leather reins are either buckled or stitched together at the centre; stitching gives a neater appearance, but otherwise there is not a great deal to choose between either, so long as the buckle tongue is in good condition.

When selecting reins for children, care should be taken with the length, as reins which are too long can easily become entangled with the rider's feet.

Plain leather reins are suitable for showing purposes, or where two reins are required, but for other activities, reins which afford better grip for the hands may be more suitable.

Plaited leather

These give good grip for hands in conditions where the reins are likely to slip through the fingers, such as when it is wet and the reins become slippery. However, they can stretch, and the plaiting eventually breaks. It is advisable to wear gloves when holding them, otherwise sore hands can result.

Laced leather

This rein also gives very good purchase for the hands. A drawback is that in order to lace the reins, large holes have to be punched down the centre through which the strips of leather which form the grips, are pulled. This makes weak spots along the rein, so extremely good observation is required if they are to be safe.

Rubber covered

These reins are particularly useful in wet conditions, or if the horse is engaged in an activity likely to make it sweat a great deal. Problems can arise from the fact that it is impossible to care properly for the leather concealed by the rubber sections, with the result that it can become very dry and brittle. This will predispose it to breaking without warning. The rubbers eventually need replacing when they wear out, but this should not be done more than twice. When the reins are taken to the saddlers for re-rubbering, hand-stitching rather than machine stitching should be requested, otherwise extra holes are created, which are likely to run into each other. When this happens, the rein is greatly weakened, and once again, there is a danger of its breaking under stress. It is always wise to take the opportunity of oiling the leather thoroughly when the rubbers have been stripped off before replacement.

16 Various types of rein

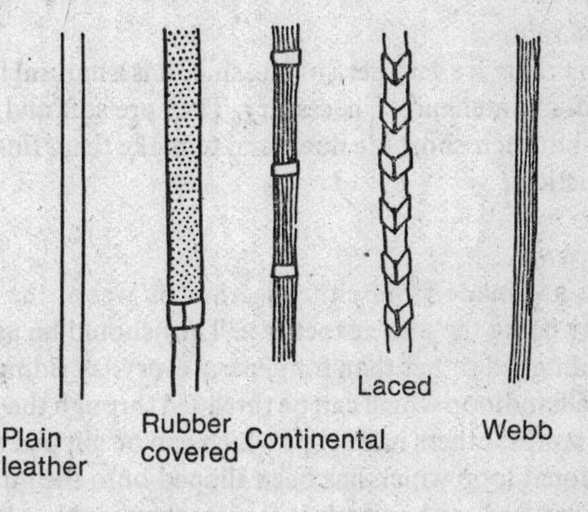

Webb or continental reins

These may be purchased with or without leather grips stitched on at regular intervals. They afford a very good purchase, especially when leather grips are included, and so are excellent for activities such as jumping, hunting, and cross country. Care should be taken to buy good quality webb, as inferior standard materials can perish very quickly. A good quality webb will have a firm feeling and a tight weave.

Nylon reins

Plaited nylon reins are popular since they are cheap to buy, strong and durable, although they are prone to stretching. It is important always to wear gloves when using reins of this type, as they can otherwise easily cause painful burns on the palms of the hands and the fingers if they are pulled away. If they stretch to a large extent, they should also be shortened, so that there is no danger of a rider's foot becoming entangled in them.

Cotton reins

Cotton reins are very perishable, since it is a natural fibre, so careful maintenance is necessary. They are soft and easy to hold, but their short life does tend to make them financially impractical.

Draw reins

These are made from either leather or webb, the leather variety being the more expensive. They should be used as a schooling aid rather than for general everyday riding. Some have a handloop which can be threaded through the girth or girth straps; others have clips which can be clipped onto an additional loop which has been slipped onto the girth. The latter method can be an advantage, as they can then be easily and quickly removed during schooling, if wished.

They may be attached in one of two different ways: firstly, from the girth on either side, passing through the bit rings and on to the rider's hands. Or an even greater degree of leverage can be created by passing them from the girth, between the horse's forelegs, through the bit rings and then to the rider's hands.

A great deal of experience and 'feel' for the way in which the horse is moving and responding is required in order to gain real benefit from their use, as it is very easy for an inexperienced rider simply to pull the animal's head into

17 Alternative positions for draw reins

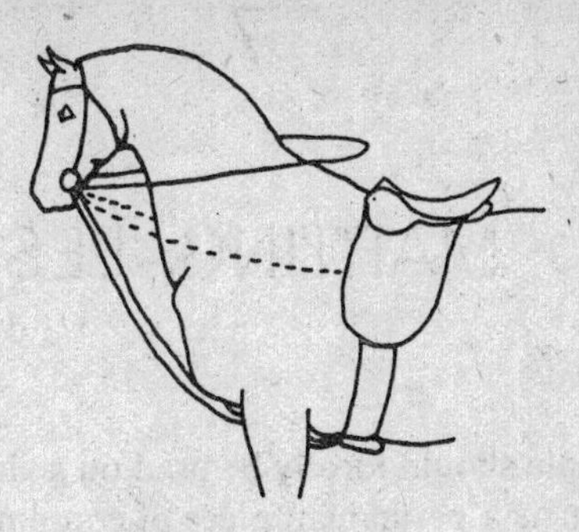

position without the necessary degree of engagement in the quarters and back, and acceptance of the bit. Certainly, somebody who has never ridden using draw reins before should not attempt to do so without initial guidance, and looking for an alternative solution first. Resistance to the bit can in fact result from their inept use, so novices should avoid them.

7

MARTINGALES

A martingale should ideally be used on a short-term basis, rather than as a permanent piece of equipment. Its action, with a few exceptions, is preventive rather than corrective, and further schooling should do away with the need for its use altogether in time. Certain types of martingale are used to assist with schooling problems, such as the Chambon and the De Gogue. These need expert supervision in their use, are beyond the sphere of everyday riding, and so are not included here.

The running, standing, bib, Irish, pulley and stretch martingales should all be used with the appropriate rein and martingale stops (see ACCESSORIES TO THE BRIDLE, Chapter 9).

Running martingale

Correctly fitted, the running martingale (fig 18) comes into action only when the head is raised above the point of control. If the horse does try to raise its head too high, a downward pressure is placed by the martingale on both reins, so that the bit exerts a stronger influence on the bars of the mouth.

Made of leather, the running martingale consists of a neckstrap with a loop in the section which rests in front of the chest. A central strap runs from the girth, passes between the front legs and through this loop in the neckstrap. It then

18 A running martingale

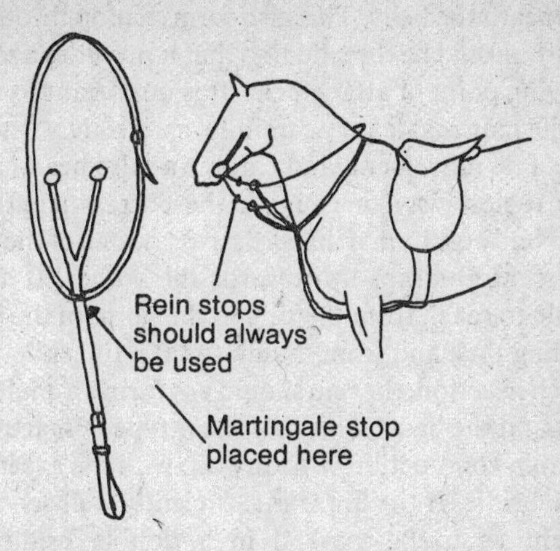

divides into two branches, with a ring on the end of each for the reins to pass through. The neckstrap is necessary to help keep the central body of the martingale in place, and to help stop it from getting entangled with the horse's legs. The neckstrap can also provide a useful emergency handhold if the rider becomes thrown off balance for some reason. Buckles should be present on the near side of the neckstrap, and also on the section passing between the front legs, so that a good fit can be obtained.

It is advisable, if buying a running martingale, to check and compare the size of the rings used on the split portion, as some rings are over-large. This in turn can lead to their slipping over the rein stops, and becoming caught up with the bit or teeth.

Fitting

The neckstrap should be adjusted by means of the buckle on the nearside so that a palm's breadth remains between the neckstrap and the point where it rests, just in front of the wither. The central strap can be adjusted using the buckle just beneath the belly. This also forms a loop through which the girth should be threaded, so that it provides a secure and unmoving point of attachment. It is important to check the fit of the martingale very carefully, as, wrongly fitted, it will restrict free movement, and enforce a false head-carriage.

The easiest way of gauging the correct length for the central body of the martingale is to draw one of the branches of the central straps up towards the wither. It should be possible to reach from the ring to the point of the wither by extending the hand from thumb to little finger.

When in action, the rein should not form an angle between the bit and the hand. This particular type of martingale can be used in conjunction with any bit, with the exception of a double bridle. If the horse is sufficiently well schooled and obedient as to be worked in a double bridle, then a martingale should not be necessary, and its effect would contradict the action of the bits anyway.

Irish martingale

The Irish martingale serves a dual purpose; to help keep rein pressure in the correct direction, and to prevent the reins from going over the horse's head should it, or the rider, fall, or if the horse is a head shaker.

It is probably the simplest of all the martingales (see fig 19) as it consists solely of a single leather strap 5″ long and ¾″ wide with a ring sewn into each end. It is most commonly seen on racehorses.

19 An Irish martingale

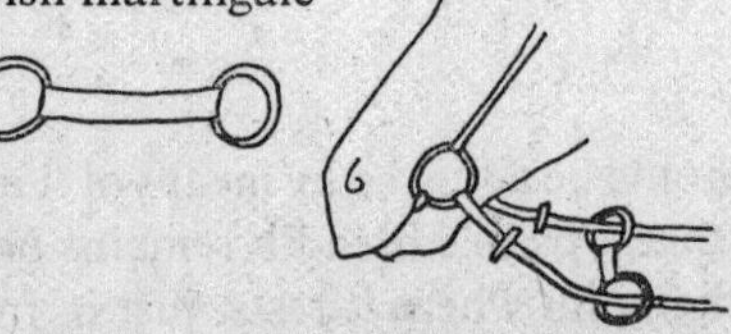

Fitting

One rein should pass through each ring. The martingale lies in front of the neck.

Bib martingale

The bib martingale is almost identical in appearance to a running martingale; the only difference being that there is a triangular 'bib' joining the two branches of the central body together. The action is the same as for the running martingale. The purpose of the 'bib' is to eliminate any danger of the horse getting caught up in the two branches, or actually biting at them.

Fitting

This martingale should be fitted as for a running martingale, although for practical purposes, it may be found necessary to have the central body shorter, if this martingale is to achieve its aims.

Standing martingale

A standing martingale should come into action only when the head is raised beyond the point of control, acting by placing pressure on the nose via the noseband. As with the running martingale, a neckstrap is necessary to hold the central strap in place (unless it is being used with a polo/Aintree type breastplate). The central strap terminates at one end in a loop through which the girth is threaded, and at the other end, in a smaller loop to accommodate the noseband. A buckle should be included in the portion of the central strap appearing above the neckstrap to allow room for adjustment to the right length. See fig 20.

20 A standing martingale

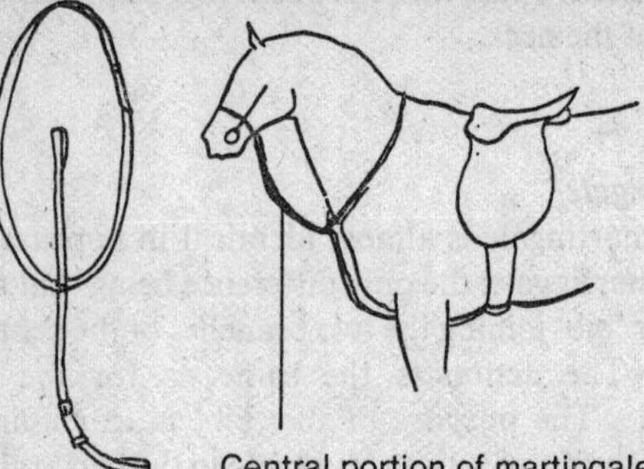

Fitting

The neckstrap is adjusted as for a running martingale. The central strap should be fitted so that it can be pushed into the contours of the lower line of the neck and jaw, when worn, although in order to be effective it does sometimes need to be slightly shorter than this. However, it should not enforce a false head-carriage, or be so short that the horse is in any way restricted, especially when jumping spread fences, where greater extension is required.

This martingale should only ever be used fastened to a snugly fitting cavesson noseband. If a dropped noseband is necessary, the problem can be solved by using a flash noseband, and attaching the standing martingale to the cavesson part of it.

Pulley martingale

This martingale is simply a refinement of the running martingale, although it is more difficult to obtain these days, and is less popular. As with the running martingale, a neckstrap with a buckle on the nearside for adjustment keeps the central body of the martingale in place. The central body is attached to the girth, passes between the front legs, and through a loop incorporated into the neckstrap at the point where it lies at the front of the chest. A small pulley is incorporated into the central body, through which a cord passes, with a ring on each end. The reins are then threaded, one through each ring, as with a running martingale.

The action is very similar to that of the running martingale, in that pressure is exerted on the bit when the head is raised above the point of control. The difference lies in the inclusion of the pulley mechanism, which allows a greater degree of lateral flexion in the neck, especially important when making sharp turns at speed, as when showjumping, for example. Because of the pulley arrangement, there is no unwanted restriction or pressure on the rein opposite to the direction of movement.

Fitting

The pulley martingale should be fitted as for a normal running martingale, except that care should be taken to ensure that an equal length of cord is kept on each side of the pulley when checking the adjustment.

Stretch martingale

This martingale was originally devised as an 'anti-rearing' device, but also serves the purpose of preventing a horse from raising its head above the point where the rider is able to control it properly. Unlike the standing martingale, which it resembles to a degree, it achieves its purpose through exerting pressure on the bit, rather than the nose, but its possible severity is lessened by the 'give' in a rubber insert in the central body.

As with most of the other martingales, a neckstrap is required, with a buckle on the nearside, to hold the central body in position, and prevent it from becoming entangled with the horse's legs. The central body attaches to the girth, passes between the front legs and up through a loop provided in the neckstrap in front of the chest. After passing through this loop, the leather terminates, and a piece of strong rubber is inserted. At the end of the strip of rubber, two short leather straps on a swivel are incorporated, with metal clips which fasten one to each bit ring.

Fitting

The neckstrap is adjusted as for the other martingales. The central body should be adjusted so that when the horse is standing naturally, there is no slack – but it must not be over-tightened, or else it will restrict the freedom of movement and cause resistance. It can be beneficial in cases where a horse hollows its back and raises its head too high in the last few strides before a fence, resulting in an awkward and uncontrolled approach and jump; but care must be exercised, both in the adjustment of this martingale for jumping, and also in not attempting to jump large fences in it, but only small ones for schooling purposes.

"*Market Harborough*"

The neckstrap ensures that the central body of the martingale remains in place. The central body attaches to the girth, passes between the front legs, and through a loop in the neckstrap in the front of the chest. Here, the leather divides into two narrower straps, each of which passes upwards and through the bit rings on either side. At the end of each division a small clip is stitched on, which is clipped to a small 'D' ring sewn onto both reins. The reins are attached to the bit as normal. See fig 21.

21 A "Market Harborough"

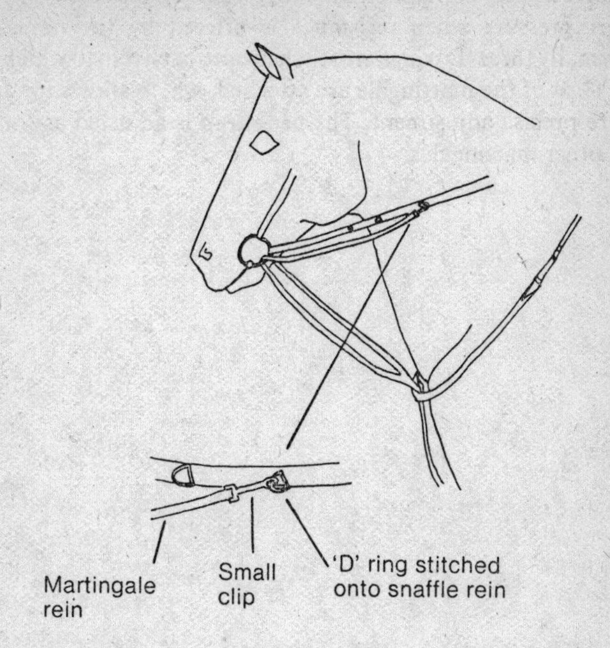

The "Market Harborough" is designed so that it should only ever come into action when the horse raises its head too high; the moment the head-carriage returns to normal, all influence by the martingale ceases. If the head is raised, the martingale straps tighten and exert a downward influence on the bit. It is particularly useful in cases where a horse not only raises its head, but becomes very strong and pulls as well.

Fitting

The martingale divisions should pass through from the inside to the outside of the bit rings. Whilst the head-carriage is correct, they should remain fairly slack, so that they only exert pressure when resistance is offered by the horse. Normally three 'D' rings are stitched onto each rein to which the clips of the martingale are attached, which allows for a more precise adjustment. The neckstrap is adjusted as for the other martingales.

8

BREASTPLATES

Breastplates are designed to help keep in place a saddle or roller which is prone to slipping backwards on a horse or pony which has poor conformation (such as narrow shoulders) or on horses which are lean because of being fit. It is an invaluable additional safety precaution to take when riding across country, or participating in any jumping activity, since it will perform the dual purpose of keeping the saddle in the correct position and provide the rider with a neckstrap to hold in an emergency. If a breastplate is regularly used, it is wise to have both a hunting and racing/polo style at hand, so that they can be alternated, so preventing chafing from occurring on the chest and shoulders.

Breastplates are generally made in one of the following patterns:

Hunting style breastplate

This type of breastplate is Y shaped, made up of a neckstrap of three pieces of leather, each connected to the other by a metal ring. The piece which passes over the top of the withers is shorter and broader than those which lie down either side of the base of the neck. These two latter straps may or may not include buckles; if they do, so much the better as adjustment is made much easier. Another strap is attached to the central ring in front of the breast, runs between the front legs and is fastened to the girth; buckles for adjustment are included, and a loop of leather to slide the girth through. A further two straps are slotted through the rings in the neckstrap either side of the withers, so that the breastplate can then be buckled to the 'D' rings on the front of saddle, holding it securely in place. See fig 22.

22 A hunting style breastplate

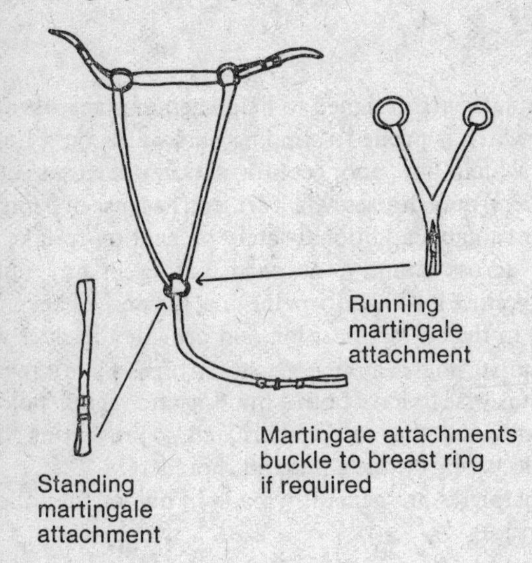

Fitting

If it is going to be of any use, the breastplate needs to be a fairly snug fit. The long sides of the neckstrap must be long enough to reach around to the front of the base of the neck. Where it passes between the front legs, the breaststrap should be adjusted so that it lies close to the skin, although not so tightly as to impede movement. Similarly, the neckstrap needs to be firmly, but not tightly, fastened. There should be no slackness in the two shorter straps which buckle onto the saddle.

Martingale attachment

If a martingale is needed, a shorter attachment can be buckled onto the central ring of the neckstrap. Either a standing or running type can be used.

Aintree and polo type breastplates

An Aintree type breastplate is made of leather with a webb front, whilst the polo type is made completely of leather, although the pattern is basically the same. Sometimes the front is covered with sheepskin to try and eliminate the likelihood of chafing. Both breastplates consist of a front breaststrap passing around the chest, which is attached to the girth on both sides by buckled leather straps. A second strap, again with buckles included for easier adjustment, is stitched into the breaststrap on either side, and runs over the neck, resting just in front of the withers. This keeps the breaststrap at the correct height, and prevents it from dropping downwards. See fig 23.

23 An Aintree or polo type breastplate

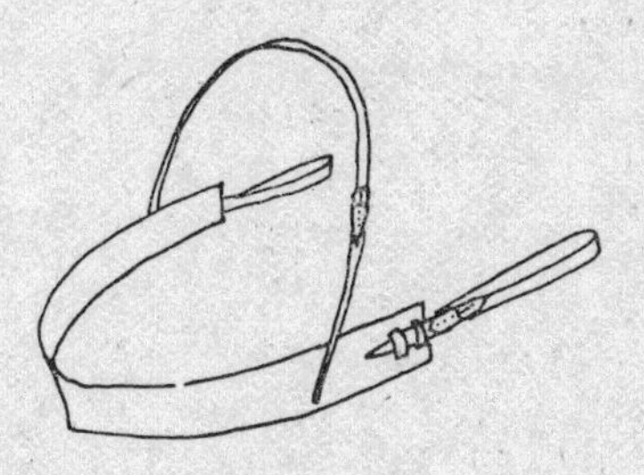

This design of breastplate is also similar to the one used for holding a roller in place over a rug, in which instance it is made of webb and leather, (see ROLLERS AND SURCINGLES, Chapter 17).

Fitting

The breastplate should be a snug, but not over-tight fit. The breaststrap should lie just beneath the base of the neck, and needs to be fitted with care since, badly adjusted, it can ride up into the neck itself and cause discomfort.

Martingale attachments

If a running or standing martingale is needed in addition to this type of breastplate, then special arrangements have to be made to accommodate it. A loop of leather or webb should be stitched into the inside and centre of the breaststrap, if there is not one already present. Then the central body of the martingale is passed through this, without the need for its normal neckstrap to hold it in place. Caution is advised when fitting the martingale, however, since it is not possible to use a rubber stop to keep the central body from looping between the front legs if it is too slack.

9

ACCESSORIES TO THE BRIDLE

Curb chains

Curb chains may be made of a variety of materials; metal links, leather, or elastic. Metal chains are of either single, double, or treble links, the single link variety being the harshest. If it is found that a single link chain cuts the jaw, then a double or treble link chain, or one made of leather or elastic could be substituted. Failing this, a rubber curb guard slipped over a metal chain will soften its effect. See fig 24. Half way along the length of all curb chains is an extra link, known as the 'fly link' through which the lip strap should be threaded. A lip strap should always be used with a curb chain, except on a Kimblewick bit, where no provision is made for its attachment. A curb chain should only ever be used with a cavesson noseband, never with one which drops beneath the bit and rests in the curb groove. Failure to observe this will result in interference in the action of both, and cause chafing.

24 (*Above*) A rubber curb guard
(*Below*) A leather curb chain

Fitting

The curb chain should be hooked over the offside hook on the bit, and passed beneath the jaw, so that it lies in the curb groove. The chain should be twisted so that it lies flat against the jaw bone, and then hooked over the nearside hook on the bit. When the shanks of the bit are drawn back to an angle of 45° to the mouth, the chain should be in contact with the jawbone; the rest of the time it should be reasonably slack.

When storing a bit which has a curb chain attached to it, it is wise to fasten the lip strap, threaded through the curb chain, as it will avoid the loss of the chain.

Lip strap

These are made of flat, or rolled, leather, and pass through the fly link of the curb chain. The purpose of a lip strap is to help keep the curb chain in the correct position on the underneath of the lower jaw, as well as to prevent the chain from turning over or becoming twisted. A twisted chain will obviously cause a great deal of pain and result in evasions.

Fitting

The end of the lipstrap which has no buckles is looped through itself on the off side of the bit, through the eyelet provided on the bit for this. The other half is buckled onto the nearside, and the same buckle used to fasten the two halves together. Having first been threaded through the fly link of the curb chain, it should be buckled up fairly loosely.

Rubber bit guards

These are round circles of rubber, with a hole in the centre, so that they can be pulled over the bit rings. When on the bit, they should lie between the corners of the mouth and the bit rings, and are used to help prevent chafing or pinching by the bit, and also to help stop the bit from being pulled through the mouth. They should not, however be used in order to replace proper schooling and correct riding, nor to alleviate a problem caused by an ill fitting or worn bit, except as a very temporary measure.

Fitting

The easiest way of placing the rings upon the bit is to pass two pieces of twine or cord through the holes. Join the ends of each piece of twine together to form two separate loops, and then place your foot through one loop of twine, and pull upwards with the other loop. This stretches the rubber to form a long slot through which the bit ring can then be inserted with the free hand. See fig 25.

25 Rubber bit guards

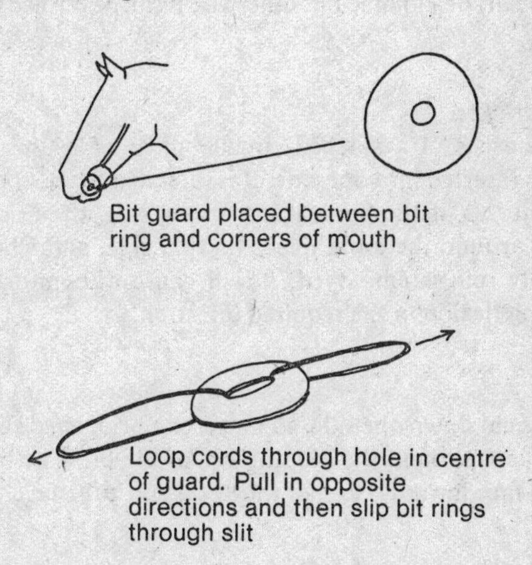

Tongue ports and grids

These take the form of either a piece of rubber attached to the centre of a bit mouthpiece, in the case of a tongue port, or a piece of wire twisted into a 'W' shape and on a separate sliphead in the case of the tongue grid. The purpose of both is to prevent a horse from placing its tongue over the bit in order to evade its action, but a metal grid, besides being more expensive, is also rather more of a mouthful.

Fitting

A metal tongue grid is attached to a separate sliphead, which should lie inside the bridle headpiece, and be buckled on the offside, so that all the buckles do not lie on one side of the face. It should be suspended slightly above the bit. The rubber tongue port is looped through itself, and should lie with the larger portion facing the rear of the horse's mouth. It is only really effective if it can be fastened around the jointed part of a jointed bit, otherwise it can be pushed to one side.

Brush pricker

This consists of a stitched circular piece of leather, with bristles inserted into one side. It is intended for use on one-sided horses; if the horse leans to one side, the pricker is placed around the mouthpiece on that side, and when the opposite rein is employed, it will cause discomfort, and resulting flexion in the required direction.

Fitting

A slit is cut down one side, so that it can be opened slightly, and placed around the mouthpiece of the bit. The bristles should face inwards, so that they lie against the face.

Martingale stop

This is made of rubber, resembling a short, stout, rubber band. It is important that it is used on any martingale (except the Irish) in order to help prevent the central body from drooping downwards between the front legs. See fig 26.

26 A martingale stop and a rein stop

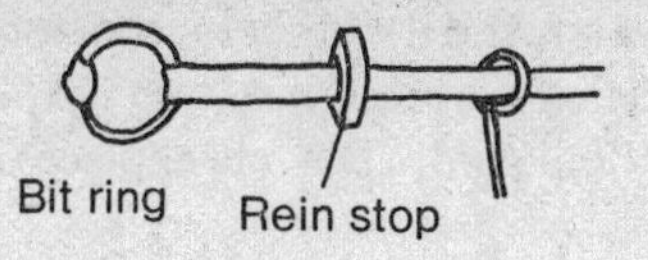

Fitting

The stop is very simply fitted, by pulling it first of all over the central body of the martingale, to the point where it intersects the neckstrap. Unbuckle the neckstrap, and then push one end of it through the stop, so that the stop lies diagonally across the two, keeping them securely in place.

Rein stops

Rein stops should always be used with running, Irish, standing, bib, and pulley martingales. They are made either of rubber, in which case they can be bought separately, and placed on each rein, or of leather, when they need to be stitched into place. It is possible to buy reins of the webbed variety with grips, which have already got such stops placed upon them. Their function is to prevent the martingale rings from sliding along the reins and becoming caught up in the bit rings. See fig 26.

Fulmer keepers

These are small strips of leather doubled over and stitched to form two loops. Their purpose is to help keep the cheekpieces of the fulmer bit in position. Being fairly small, they are very easy to lose when stripping a bridle down, so if a particular bridle is only ever used with a fulmer bit, it can be a good idea to have them stitched into the cheekpiece. See fig 27.

Fitting

The keepers are fitted so that one loop passes over the top cheekpiece of the fulmer bit, and the other loop is fastened to the bridle cheekpiece, so that it is positioned over the platform between keeper and hookstud. The cheekpiece is then fastened as normal.

Pelham roundings

These are made of sturdy rolled leather, and are bought in pairs. A small buckle is stitched into each end for attachment to the bit. Keep a careful eye on them, as they take a lot of strain and the leather has been made thinner in order to roll it, and so is not as strong as a piece of plain leather. The moment any weaknesses are noticed, the roundings should be replaced with new ones. See fig 27.

27 A Fulmer keeper and a Pelham rounding

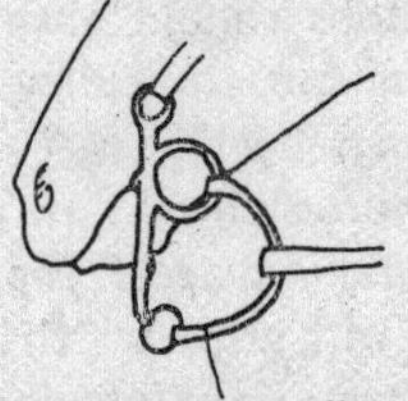

Fitting

One end is attached to the snaffle ring on the Pelham bit, and the other end attached to the bottom ring on the bit. The reins are then fastened around the rolled section of leather. This method enables a novice rider to use only one pair of reins instead of two, although it means that the curb action is always in play; with two pairs of reins it is possible to use more curb or snaffle as desired. It can also be a useful arrangement for a young rider with small hands and a strong pony, giving greater control whilst avoiding the complexities and larger handful of two sets of reins.

10

HEADCOLLARS

The term 'headcollar' covers more than simply headcollars; it also includes such items as lead reins, muzzles, crib straps and so forth.

Headcollars

These are made of leather or nylon, with brass, nickel, or cadmium-plated furniture. Headcollars are used when handling horses or ponies in the stable, when leading out, tying up, etc. They should not be left on if it can be avoided, as they may get caught up in stable fittings or tree branches. Whatever the type of headcollar it should be fairly sturdy and strong, since it will suffer much wear and tear and rough treatment.

There are two main types of headcollar – the 'Yearling' pattern and the 'Albert' pattern. See fig 28. A 'Yearling' headcollar has buckles on the noseband and throatlash as well as on the near side of the headpiece. This allows a great deal of adjustment so that plenty of room for growth is possible. The 'Albert' headcollar has a buckle on both sides of the headpiece and is generally of much stouter workmanship. Traditionally, a browband should come as part and parcel of such a headcollar, but with the rising cost of leather nowadays, this does not always follow.

28 Headcollars

'Yearling' pattern

'Albert' pattern

A headcollar is made up of a number of pieces of leather or nylon joined by metal squares and rings and buckles to form the whole. The parts of the headcollar are as follows: noseband, two jowl pieces, backstay, throatpiece, (of rounded leather in 'Albert' pattern) two cheekpieces and a headpiece. Leather headcollars are normally stitched up using two rows of stitching, but in the smarter type, three rows may be used instead. This will be more expensive to buy because of the extra labour involved. Whenever brass furniture is used, the stitching will be yellow in colour to match, rather than white.

Fitting

The headcollar should be a snug fit – if it is too large, there is a danger of its being slipped off, or of the horse's foot being caught up in it. If a buckle is present on the noseband, check to ensure that it is mounted on leather or nylon, otherwise it will be in direct contact with the nose and will rub badly.

Foal headcollars

These are made of leather or nylon, and are a lighter, finer version of the 'Yearling' pattern headcollars. They should be softer also, as the foal's face is more delicate than that of an older animal. Many people put one on and leave it on from several days after birth, but this is not wise as the foal may become entangled with objects in the field or stable. It is more sensible simply to make a habit of putting it on each day whilst handling the foal, and then removing it.

It sometimes includes a 'hand tab' – or short piece of leather or nylon attached to the back ring of the noseband.

Fitting

They should be a close snug fit, although not so tight as to cause discomfort or rubbing.

Dutch slip

This consists of two pieces of soft leather crossing one over the other so as to form a figure eight, and held in position by two cheekstraps. It is usually cheap and light for a foal to wear, but not ideal as it tends to slip into the eyes.

Fitting

Should be a snug, comfortable fit.

Halters

Halters are made of hemp or cotton webb, and are a cheap alternative to headcollars. They consist of a loop of webb, terminating in a rope. A woven eyelet is incorporated into the webb so that the rope can be passed beneath the jaw and threaded through the eyelet and knotted. It must be a fixed knot rather than a slip knot which could tighten on the nose. The real problem with halters is that they rot quickly and do not always fit very well; they often slip into the eyes.

Lead reins

These are made from cotton, nylon, leather or cotton/polyester.

Cotton tubular webb or leather are normally used when showing. Often they have a 'Newmarket' chain on the end, terminating in a brass clip. The chain is made of brass or is brass plated, and about 18" long. The alternative to this is to have a leather billet with a brass buckle fastening. A 'billet' is a means of attaching one piece of saddlery to another – by buckles or hook studs or clips. There is no hand loop, but the end is tapered so that it is easier to hold. They should be at least 6 feet long in case of a horse or pony rearing; if a stallion is being led, then it should be at least 10 feet long and have a brass chain. Nylon lead reins sometimes have a handloop, which can be dangerous if it is used. It is better to tie a knot in the end to give better grip rather than risk the hand becoming trapped in it. The other end terminates in either a trigger or spring clip. Gloves should always be worn when leading with any type of lead rein, but it is especially important with nylon ones. They are very slippery and difficult to hold, and if they do slip, will burn the palms of hands which are not protected.

Cotton/polyester ropes either have a woven eyelet so that they can be looped through the headcollar and through the eyelet, or else have spring, trigger, or quick release clips.

Fitting

Lead reins should be attached to the back ring or square of the headcollar to ensure proper control. If a spring clip is used, the clip opening should face away from the jawbone so that in the event of a horse or pony moving abruptly backwards it will not cause an injury. If the rein is attached to a bridle, it should be fastened to the noseband, or passed through the nearside bit ring and fastened to the offside bit ring. When tying up, a quick release knot (see fig 29) should always be used, and the lead rein tied to a piece of string rather than to an immovable object. In the event of an emergency, the string will then break, rather than the rein, or headcollar, and before injuries can be caused to the animal.

In hand couples

More frequently seen these days are approximately 8″ long 'Newmarket' chains made of brass, or brass plated, with a clip at each end, and a brass ring in the centre. They are used when leading and showing young stock, stallions and broodmares.

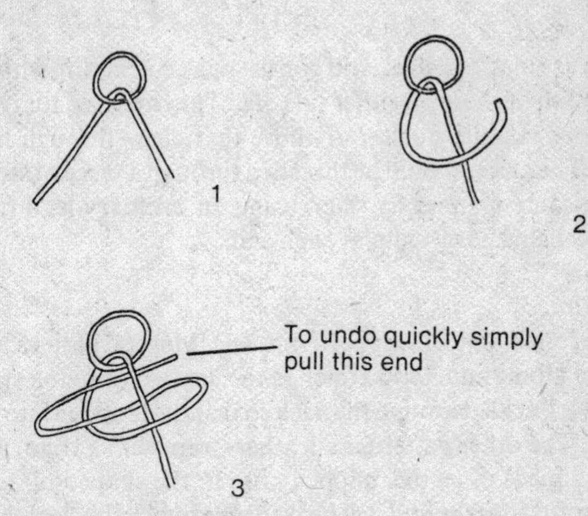

29 (*Above*) Three stages in tying a quick release knot
(*Below*) A three-way couple

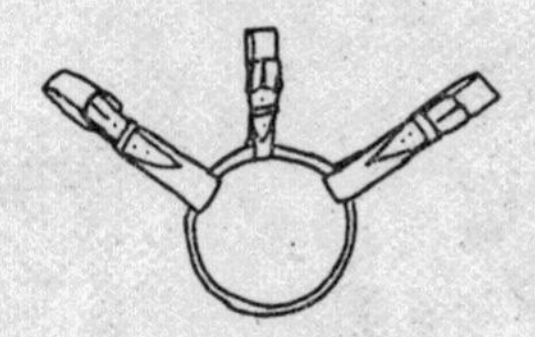

Fitting

The clips fasten one to each bit ring, and the lead rein fastens onto the brass ring in the centre. The sort of lead rein used should be one with a 'Newmarket' chain incorporated into it.

Three way couples

This consists of a large brass ring with three straps leading from it. Two of the straps buckle onto the bit rings, whilst the third is buckled onto a 'D' on the back of the bridle noseband. The lead rein then fastens onto the brass ring. See fig 29.

Rack chains

These are made of steel, and consist of a central ring with an 18″ length of chain on either side of it. They are used for tying up more volatile horses, or those that chew through lead reins. The chain should be threaded through a piece of string in the same manner as when using an ordinary lead rein. These chains have a clip at each end.

Crib straps

These follow one of two patterns. The 'Meyers' pattern, is a hinged aluminium loop attached to a leather or nylon strap which is buckled around the neck so that the loop fits into the gullet. The other pattern is a leather strap, with a triangular shaped piece of leather slipped onto it; the shaped piece of leather fits into the gullet. The principle behind both of these straps is to prevent crib biting and windsucking; the 'Meyers' pattern appears to be more effective. See fig 30.

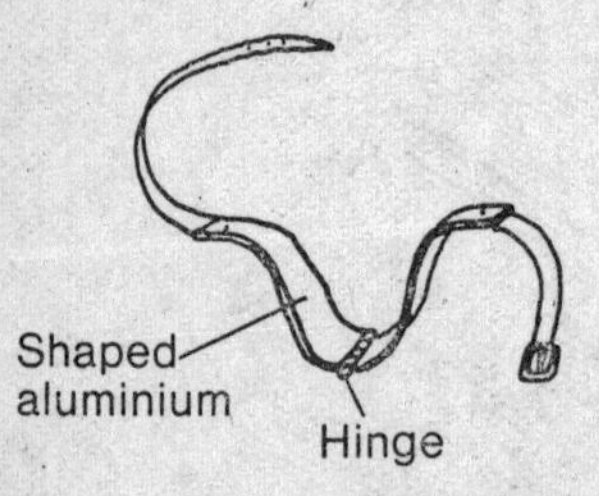

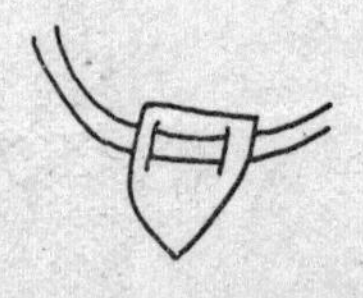

30 Crib straps: (*Left*) A 'Meyers' pattern (*Right*) A leather strap

Fitting

Both straps need to be fitted quite firmly if they are to prove at all effective.

Fly fringes

These are effective in keeping flies away from the eyes during the summer, especially if the forelock is very sparse. The drawback is that a headcollar needs to be left on all the time to provide a way of attaching them. They are made of string, nylon, leather, vinyl, material, or a combination of these. They consist of a browband with strips of whichever material is used hanging down from it. See fig 31.

31 A fly fringe

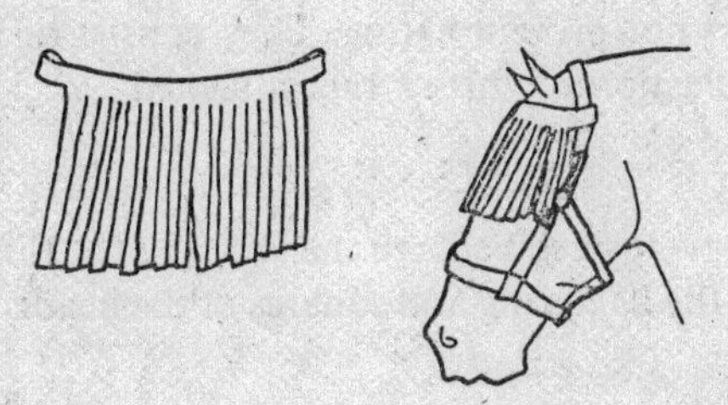

Muzzles

These are used to prevent biting, eating droppings and bedding, or to prevent eating when at competitions. They are made of leather or plastic, resembling a bucket which fits around the muzzle. Two large holes are provided for the nostrils, and a number of smaller ones in the bottom, so that it is lighter and the horse is able to drink. The plastic variety are more practical, since they can be easily cleaned, but can rub around the top if they are badly finished. See fig 32.

32 A clothing bib (*left*) and a muzzle (*right*)

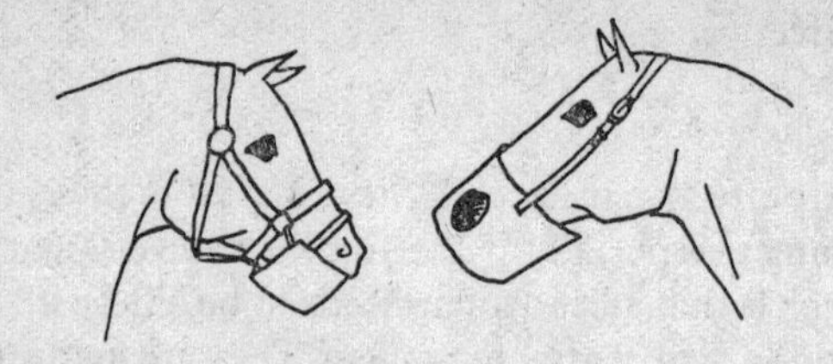

Fitting

The strap attached to the muzzle should be passed over the poll and buckled on the nearside so that it is a close fit.

Clothing bibs

These are used for preventing rug tearing, but unlike muzzles, do not prevent eating. They consist of a flap of leather or plastic with three straps attached.

Fitting

The flap is positioned beneath the jaw, and the three straps buckled to the back ring and squares of the headcollar. See fig 32.

In hand bridle

An in hand bridle is basically like a riding bridle. The noseband does not have a separate headpiece, but slips through the cheekpieces of the bridle. The throatlash usually has a buckle on both sides. Buckles are normally used instead of hook stud fastenings, and these are of brass. Whole rather than half buckles are traditional, with yearling and two year old fillies wearing rounded rather than square buckles. Two year old fillies can also be shown in bitless in hand bridles.

Stallions have brass side mountings on bits, brass browbands and brass rosettes at the ends of the browband.

Whilst stallions wear a straight bar bit, colts and broodmares may wear whatever snaffle bit is most suitable. Sometimes a brass 'D' is stitched into the back of the bridle noseband to lead from, instead of, or as well as, the bit. See fig 33.

33 Stallion in hand bridle

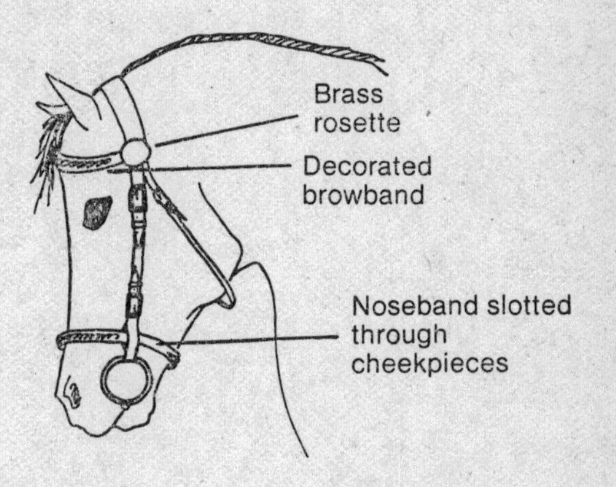

Bitless in hand bridles have a normal riding bridle type headpiece, which may or may not have buckles on both sides of the throatlash according to taste. The cheekpieces drop down to what is essentially the front part of a dropped noseband, that ends in a ring on either side. From there it is the handler's choice as to how to lead – either with couples clipped to the rings, or a lead rein slipped through them.

All in hand bridles have stitched nosebands. The browband should relate to the type of animal being shown; for example, a small show pony should have a velvet browband, a Welsh cob a brass one, and a riding horse a plain one.

Fillies and geldings of three years of age should be shown in an ordinary riding snaffle bridle, whilst older horses being shown in hand should wear a double bridle. Yearling fillies and foals can be shown in headcollars if wished.

11

LUNGING EQUIPMENT

Lunging can be a useful skill to acquire, although a novice intending to exercise a horse or pony in this way should first try to obtain some tuition from an experienced person. Once proficient, lunging can be used for several reasons; exercising a horse or pony which is over-fresh before riding it, or if it cannot be ridden due to galls or similar injury. Another use is when teaching a rider, as exercises can be performed which are not possible when riding independently, although the animal used should obviously be steady and reliable. It is also an excellent way of teaching a young horse to jump, since there is no rider to interfere with its freedom of movement. Lunging is also the first work which a young horse performs before being backed and ridden away, instilling obedience to the commands and building up muscle and suppleness before a rider's weight is placed upon it.

Before attempting lunging, it is advisable to obtain some suitable equipment in order to ensure proper control and safety, both for the horse or pony and the handler.

Lunging cavesson

These are made in nylon webb or leather, but the most important point is that they should be of stout workmanship and materials. The patterns vary somewhat, but the better type will allow for adjustment on both sides of the headpiece, rather than just on one side. This ensures that the jowl strap does not end up unnecessarily high; certainly it should not be allowed to ride up where it can press against the gullet and cause discomfort. The headpiece is buckled to cheekpieces on either side, which are in turn stitched onto a padded noseband. The noseband must be fastened very firmly so that it does not move around on the nose when the lunge rein is attached to it, or sores could be caused. A metal plate is attached to the front of the noseband, usually by means of small leather straps. The plate should ideally be made of steel; lighter cavessons employ aluminium or cheap alloys, but these materials tend to be brittle and break under heavy strain. The plate should be hinged in three places. Although cavessons are often seen with only one hinge in the centre, these can pinch the nose, especially on animals with coarser heads, and never seem to fit really snugly.

Three rings mounted on swivels are normally placed on the plate, which is a much more satisfactory arrangement than the type which have only one, or fixed, rings. The swivels help to prevent the lunge rein from becoming twisted, and with difficult horses, the additional ring on either side of the central one allows for variation in the position of the lunge rein. They can also be used for sidereins, when these are being introduced initially to a young horse.

Either a throatlash or a jowl strap, or sometimes both, are stitched onto the head or cheekpieces of the cavesson. If the jowl strap is present, the throatlash is unnecessary, and indeed, should not be overtightened as it could interfere with respiration and cause discomfort. A browband is sometimes included when buying a cavesson, but is not really necessary, and can be disposed of if desired. See fig 34.

Fitting

The noseband part of the cavesson should be fitted at the same height as an ordinary bridle cavesson noseband, and must be fastened fairly tightly so that it does not slip and lead

34 A lunging cavesson

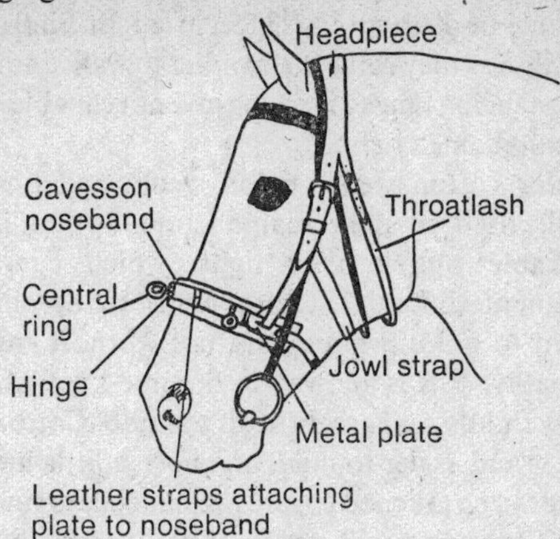

to chafing. The jowl strap should be fastened as firmly as possible beneath the jaw and just in front of the cheekbone. Its purpose is to prevent the cheekpieces from riding upwards into the eyes. If a throatlash is present, it should be fastened so as to allow a palm's breadth between it and the gullet.

When being used with a bridle, the noseband should pass beneath the bridle cheekpieces so that interference with the bit does not occur when the sidereins are attached. The jowl strap and throatlash will be found to sit more comfortably if they are passed over the top of the bridle cheekpieces. When fitting a bridle and cavesson together, the bridle should be put on first, the cavesson second, and the bridle noseband removed, so that it does not get in the way of the lunging cavesson. If the horse tries to evade the bit by opening its mouth, a dropped noseband fitted to the bridle does not usually interfere with the fitting of the lunging cavesson; or else a lunging cavesson can be bought which has a dropping back strap. It can then be adjusted to fit in the same manner as a dropped noseband.

Lunge rein

This should be of about 18–23 feet in length. Shorter ones are undesirable as they force the handler to walk a small circle if the animal being lunged is young and not capable of working on a small diameter circle.

Tubular cotton webb, nylon webb, and linen are the materials used in their manufacture. Nylon is virtually unbreakable but is very light, which can make its management difficult. It also tends to be slippery and awkward to hold; if gloves are not worn, it can burn the palms badly. If it is allowed to become knotted, the knots pull very tightly and are difficult to undo. Cotton and linen are softer and easier to hold, and have a little more weight. Care should be taken to ensure regular checks since these are natural fibres and will perish easily, especially if kept in damp conditions.

A loop is normally made at one end, although the hand should not be pushed through it in case the horse or pony pulls away and the hand becomes trapped. Better grip can be gained by tying a knot in the end of the lunge rein and holding that instead.

The lunge rein is attached to the cavesson with either a spring clip, trigger clip, or a leather strap and buckle fastening. This last has disadvantages in that the swivel is usually so far away from the end that it can hit the horse's face if it tosses its head. A spring clip is probably the easiest method of the three. The swivels on all these fastenings should be regularly oiled to keep them efficient.

Sidereins

Sidereins are either elasticated, or plain with no give in them at all. Stretch is provided by including a section of strong surgical elastic, or alternatively a rubber ring. See fig 35. It is a matter of personal preference which sort is used, as both have their advantages and disadvantages. Elasticated sidereins are more expensive, and, if elastic is used, it eventually has to be replaced when the stretchiness has gone. Some schools of thought prefer them as the 'give' imitates that of the rider's hand, whilst others say that they can encourage a horse to lean on them, or to draw back behind the rein contact.

35 Sidereins

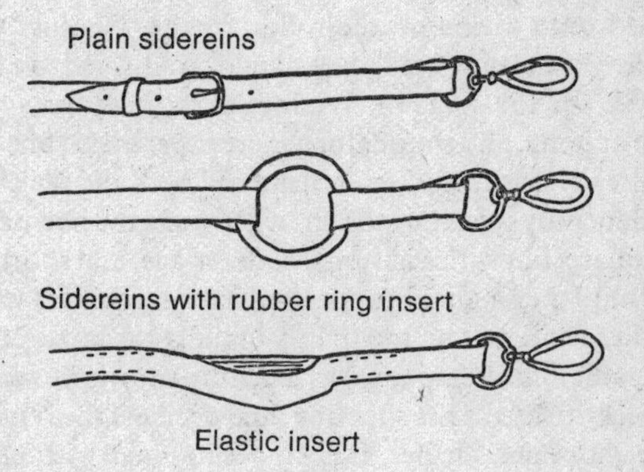

Sidereins are most frequently made in leather, although nylon webb is obtainable. Their purpose is to replace the rider's normal rein contact, and to help keep the horse moving as straight as possible. At one end is a spring or trigger clip which can be snapped onto the lunging cavesson noseband rings, or onto the bit. At the other end is either a plain leather loop, or another set of clips which can be attached to the saddle or lunging roller. Adjustment to the length is made by means of a buckle in the centre.

Fitting

The sidereins can be attached either to the rings on a lunging roller, or the girth straps of the saddle. The more advanced the horse or pony in its training, the higher the reins can be positioned, whilst with a novice animal, they are positioned much lower. This is because a more advanced animal works with a higher headcarriage than a novice one; sidereins too low will imbalance it and hold back further improvement in its work.

When not in use, the sidereins should not be left clipped onto the bit rings, either when the horse is standing still, or being led, as this can lead to evasions of the bit. They can be clipped onto a ring on the roller, or the 'D' rings of the saddle. When being used, they should be adjusted to a length suitable for the stage of training; fairly long for a young horse or pony, and shorter for a more experienced one which has already learnt to lower its head and neck and seek for the bit. Generally speaking, to start with, stand the horse so that it is square, but with a natural headcarriage, and shorten the reins until they maintain a constant but light contact with the bit. If they are put on too tightly initially the horse or pony may panic and attempt to rear. Once the horse is moving, it is then easy to assess the situation, and decide if the reins need to be shortened further. It is kinder to lunge without side-reins for the first few minutes anyway, so that the horse or pony has a chance to stretch and relax first before settling down to more serious work.

Both sidereins should be kept at the same height on both sides of the body, and be shortened to the same length, so that an even contact is placed on the mouth or nose. Shortening one rein more than the other is sometimes necessary with certain problem horses, but should really only be undertaken by an experienced trainer who understands the effects that this creates.

Lunging roller

The lunging roller, (to which the sidereins are attached when a saddle is not being used) is made of either leather or hemp webb, and the best sorts are divided into two sections so that they can be adjusted on both sides. A padded section should be included where it passes over the back, so that there is no direct pressure on the spine. Rings are stitched into the roller at intervals on both sides, so that the height of the sidereins can be varied. Another 'D' ring should be included at the centre and back of the roller, so that a crupper (see page 110) can be added, to prevent the roller from being pulled forwards once the sidereins are attached.

The roller is usually introduced before the saddle when training the young horse or pony, since it moves around less on the back, and is less likely to incur damage should the animal panic. If two larger rings are stitched into the roller, it can then also be used for long reining, since the two reins can be passed through them.

Lunging whip

A long lunging whip is necessary when working a horse or pony on the lunge, and together with the voice, replaces the rider's normal leg signals. It should be used to encourage the horse to move forward, rather than to strike it, although an occasional flick may be necessary with a lazy animal.

The most commonly available, and cheapest sort has a fibreglass stock with a long plaited nylon thong. This thong often frays at the end of the stock, but a piece of sticking plaster or insulating tape wrapped around this area will help to extend its life. A fibreglass whip such as this is light and easy to handle, and so ideal for its purposes.

Long reins

If necessary, two lunge reins will suffice, although long leather reins are more pleasant to hold and less easily tangled. They have either a stud hook fastening to the bit, or a spring clip. The latter should be mounted on a swivel, and will help to stop the reins getting twisted. Long reins are the next step after lunging for a young horse, teaching it the rudiments of steering. Later, quite advanced work can be performed with them.

Fitting

The stud hook or clip fastening should be attached either to the side rings of the lunging cavesson, or directly to the bit rings, according to the level of training of the horse. The reins should then be threaded through the rings on a lunging roller. Alternatively, a saddle may be used, and the reins passed through the stirrup irons, which should first have been secured to the girth with a spur strap to stop them from moving about.

12

SADDLES

The saddle is usually the most expensive single item of saddlery bought by a horse owner. This is not just because of the large amount of leather used – in some cases vinyl replaces parts of the flaps and panels in order to keep prices as low as possible – but because of the time required by a craftsman to make one. Although some stages can be completed with the aid of machinery, the bulk of the work can only be done by hand.

Saddle tree

The framework of the saddle is the saddle tree itself. This is usually made of beechwood. Experiments have been made using fibreglass as a substitute but these were largely unsuccessful, except for use in racing saddles, and so the traditional wooden materials have remained. Since it is wood, it is prone to stresses and breaks, and so the saddle should always be handled with care. Dropping a saddle not only damages the finish on the leather, but can smash the tree inside, ruining it permanently, or at best involving expensive repairs, if indeed a saddler can be found who will take the job on!

Trees are called either spring trees, or rigid trees; if the former, the saddle is usually stamped to this effect on the panel. Rigid trees are more substantial to look at than the more modern spring tree; the latter gains its name from the two strips of steel running from the underside of the front arch to the cantle. This allows for a deeper and shorter seat, so that the rider cannot move about so much and interfere with the action of the horse's back muscles. It is a great deal more comfortable for the rider than the older, flatter, rigid tree. See fig 1, page 23.

The head of the tree is either vertical, or is set back at a slope – termed a 'cut back head'. Most modern spring tree saddles have a cut back head regardless of whether it is really necessary or not. The object of it is to allow for clearance of the withers, especially in instances where the withers are not only high, but lacking in muscle on either side to hold the saddle.

Most saddles with spring trees also have what are known as 'flexible points'. The points are at the end of the saddle head, and in older saddles were long and unyielding, so that the saddle could only be used on a limited number of horses. In modern trees, the points are much shorter, and terminate in pieces of leather (hence the 'flexible' points) so that saddle fitting is much easier. The shorter points also have the advantage in that they do not cause an uncomfortable lump beneath the rider's thigh. The points can be seen lying in a 'point pocket' when the saddle flaps are lifted up. These are situated at the top of the knee rolls, and in front of the girth straps.

The stirrup bars should have the word 'forged' or 'cast' stamped on them – if not, they should be viewed with suspicion as being an inferior, possibly unsafe product, probably of Indian origin. The bars should be inclined very slightly upwards, so that the stirrup leathers do not slip off accidentally, and also should be close to the tree. A loose bar, or one which does not fit snugly into the rest of the saddle, should be viewed with suspicion; it could mean that the tree is damaged.

At the end of each stirrup bar is a hinged catch known as

the 'thumbpiece'. This can be left in the up or down position. The theory behind it is that the catch should be left up, but should the rider fall, and a foot become trapped in the stirrup iron, the stirrup leather pulls the catch down, and the leather is released. In reality, most catches are far too stiff to perform this function, and it is safer to leave it down permanently. See fig 36.

The stirrup bars themselves are riveted to the tree, either on top or underneath. The former arrangement means that if the bar is not shaped, it stands a little proud of the finished saddle, and can be uncomfortable to ride in.

A point to be made in favour of rigid trees is that, although less comfortable and with a flatter seat and fewer of the luxuries of a spring tree saddle, they often prove to be the better workhorse, especially in an environment such as a riding school or trekking centre. This is mainly because they are not prone to the distortions that can arise with a spring tree. If a rider mounts badly in a spring tree saddle – holding the pommel and cantle, for example – it can twist the waist of the tree (see fig 1, page 23), so that it then becomes uncomfortable for the horse to wear. After a period of about five years, the springs are reckoned to become weaker, and so it is silly to buy a secondhand spring tree saddle older than this. Trees are made in a number of sizes, ranging anywhere from around twelve inches in length to eighteen or perhaps more. Up to sixteen inches in length is suitable for children, and longer than that for adults, depending upon physical build.

Trees also come in different width fittings – narrow, wide, and medium. Some companies number the widths of trees, and can also supply a saddle with an 'open' or 'closed' tree so that the best fit possible can be ensured. The standard widths (i.e. narrow, medium or wide) are stretched or compressed in a vice to adjust them to 'open' or 'closed' (wider or narrower) fittings – this can weaken the tree.

36 Two views of a general purpose saddle

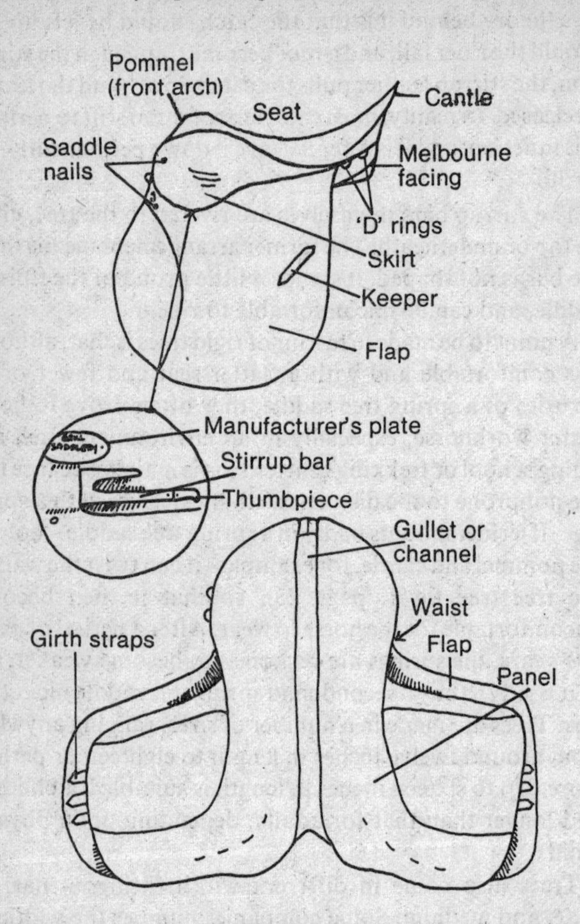

When measuring the length of a finished saddle, the measurement can be taken using a piece of string stretched tautly from one of the saddle nails on the pommel to the very centre of the cantle. Remember that the saddle should fit the horse's back as well as the rider's seat.

Girth webbs

All quality saddles should have two separate pieces of webb running across the seat to which the girth straps can be attached. The first girth strap is usually attached to the first piece of webb, and the second and third girth straps stitched to the second, wider piece of webb. The webb itself may be canvas, or more frequently seen nowadays, nylon.

Often, when a saddle is taken apart, it is found that these pieces of webb do not stretch right across the saddle; they are cut short, and just tacked onto the tree. Such an arrangement is not so safe, as the webb is likely to fray around the tacks, and eventually pull free. If the webb is stretched over the seat as well, with just a few tacks to stop it from moving around, there is less chance of a nasty accident happening before the fraying is noticed. Signs of such wear should be looked for when buying a secondhand saddle, and if noticed, it should be taken to a saddler and new webbs put in immediately.

At least one of the girth straps should be stitched onto a separate webb, since it is a safety precaution. In the event of one webb breaking, at least there will be another to which the girth is fastened, to stop it from becoming unexpectedly detached. Indian saddles often have all the girth straps stitched onto the same piece of webb; many only have two girth straps anyway. Dressage saddles that only have two long girth straps frequently are only stitched onto one piece of webb also. Although more energetic and dangerous activities such as jumping or hunting are unlikely to be carried out in such saddles, a nasty fall could still result if this single webb broke.

Panels

The panel is the name given to the padded underpart of the saddle. It is divided into two halves which sit one on either side of the backbone, so that the rider's weight is taken onto the muscles on both sides, and not directly onto the spine.

The gap between the two panels is called the 'gullet' or 'channel', and when carefully inspected should not dramatically narrow at the waist of the saddle or bow outwards. These occurrences could result in pinching of the backbone, or uneven weight distribution and sores. Similarly, the size of the panels should be compared; they should be as equal as possible in size and shape, with the same amount of padding in both. Saddles which fail these tests are usually the result of companies producing large quantities of cheap apprentice-made saddles; they will result in poor and uneven weight distribution, and place the rider in a crooked position. Such flaws, when discovered, are almost impossible to correct.

Panels are either 'full' or 'half' panels. The latter sort are most often seen on children's saddles. They allow for a very close leg contact with the pony's sides, but lack the security given by a knee roll. Half panels cut the final cost of the saddle, since less leather is needed for their manufacture. Some ponies, due to their shape, can be very difficult to fit a full panelled saddle to, and a half panel can be the solution. Where a half panel is present, there should be an additional 'sweat flap' – a piece of leather stitched to the girth webbs, and hanging between the girth straps and the panel. When the girth is fastened, the buckles then lie on these sweat flaps, so that no pinching or rubbing is caused. See fig 37.

Full panels have knee rolls or knee and thigh rolls fitted to them. The former is known as a 'Saumur' panel, and the latter a 'Continental' panel. See fig 38. The knee roll gives greater security in the saddle, especially when jumping. A thigh roll, when added, should not be over-large as it tends to fix the rider's leg position, not always in the right place. Where activities such as dressage are involved, it may be better to avoid a thigh roll altogether, as it can impede the development of a longer leg. Thigh rolls were initially introduced so that the girth straps did not slip backwards off the panel; but if this is likely to happen, then the design of the saddle itself is at fault.

37 A half panelled saddle

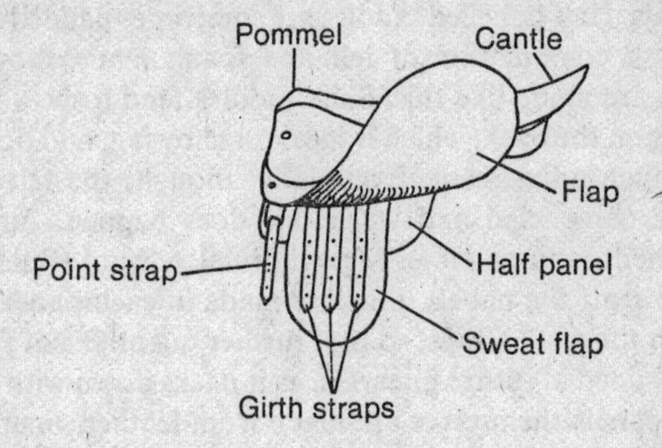

38 Two types of full panel saddle

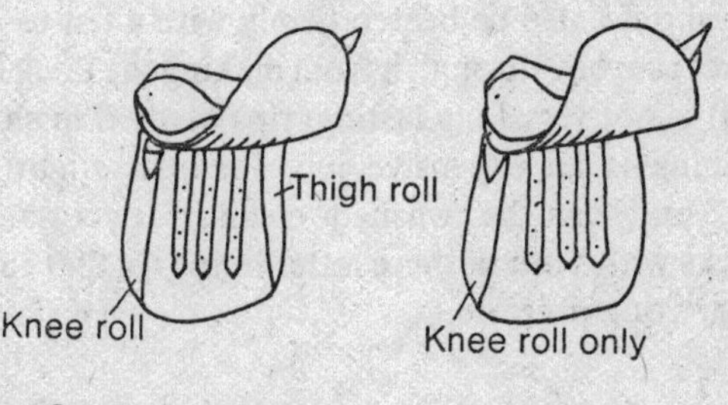

Spring trees usually have shorter and deeper seats than rigid trees, which can make equal weight distribution along the length of the saddle difficult to achieve. In some cases the saddle is actually seen to 'rock' on the horse's back. To encourage a more correct weight distribution and better fit, 'Melbourne facings' are sometimes inserted into the back of the panel as shown in fig 36 on page 98.

Panels are made from, and padded with, different materials. Half panelled saddles are sometimes padded with felt, or a combination of felt and foam; many showing saddles are made like this. Such saddles tend to be a very close fit on the back, which is ideal for showing, and do not need much adjustment. Eventually, though, the felt will become compacted and when this does happen, further adjustment is impossible. More normally, wool (flock) is used to stuff the panels. Slits are made in each panel just beneath the girth straps, so that further quantities of flock can be added at future intervals, as it packs down with use.

The panels themselves are made from leather, linen, or serge. Leather is probably the most popular, if most expensive of these. However, it is durable, and easy to clean. Serge and linen are more likely to be found on old rigid tree saddles than on modern saddles. Serge is a woollen material, which should be brushed each time after use, once it has dried. It should also be beaten firmly with a fist to prevent the sweat absorbed through it from making the flock become lumpy. It is not very long lasting, rips easily if mishandled, and relining is an expensive job. Linen is slightly more durable, and can be washed clean if necessary. The drawbacks with both of these latter linings is that they take time to dry out after use.

Flaps

The flaps of the saddle cover the panel and girth straps, protecting the rider's legs against the latter. Some flaps have suede or hide covering the knee roll, supposedly to assist grip when jumping. In reality, they do not help a great deal, but can be the source of problems as they wear. The suede quickly loses its finish, whilst both materials will also wear through quickly. Unsightly holes are then left. The stitching wears quickly as well, necessitating frequent repairs. Any saddle which is hide covered on the seat and flaps will suffer in the same way, and so is not always an ideal investment.

Types of saddle

The types of saddle most likely to be in demand by the average horse owner include the general purpose (GP) saddle, jumping, dressage, showing, and felt pad. The differences are shown in fig 39.

The general purpose saddle is probably the most favoured and widely sold of all these designs. It is intended to allow the rider to participate in all activities, from flatwork to jumping, allowing the rider to sit in a safe and effective position throughout. A well-designed saddle should encourage the rider to sit squarely over the horse's centre of balance, without fixing or displacing the rider's leg position. Some saddles, although described as general purpose, are geared quite strongly towards jumping, with a very forward cut flap to accommodate the shorter length of stirrup. This is not ideal, and will make activities on the flat more difficult for the rider. A good general purpose saddle is one which is not too extreme in its cut or style.

Jumping saddles are designed specifically for the purpose of jumping. They have forward cut flaps to this purpose, so that the rider can shorten the stirrups without the knee extending over the front of the flap. These flaps can sometimes present problems when fitting the saddle, as they can interfere with the movement of the shoulder. The seat is usually fairly deep, and slightly longer than in a general purpose, and knee and thigh rolls are often included on the panels.

Dressage saddles are intended for use during flatwork. They have a very much straighter cut flap, since the rider should be sitting deep in the seat with the leg long so that as

39 Various types of saddle

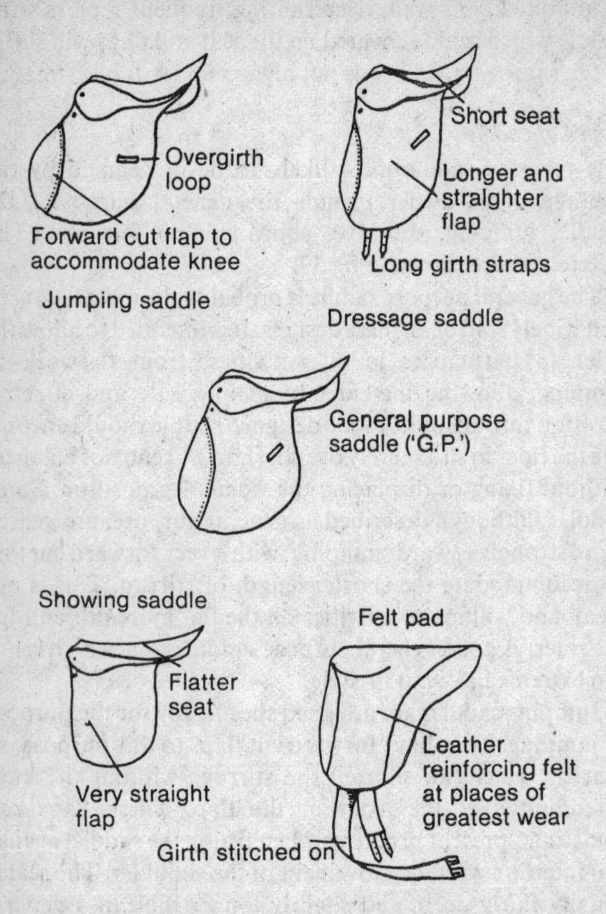

much of it as possible is in contact with the horse's sides. The straightness of the flaps helps to keep the rider's leg positioned directly beneath the seat, as well as long. The seats of such saddles are normally deep, and quite short, with a narrow waist. This all helps the rider to sit in an effective position and as close to the horse as possible with the seat and legs.

Showing saddles are designed more with a view to showing off a horse or pony than with an eye to the rider's comfort. They are very straight cut, almost to the extent that the front line of the flap is behind the vertical. The total area of the saddle tends to be small, since the object is to allow as much of the horse or pony to be seen as possible. They are also very flat in the seat, which, together with the design of the flap, does little to make the rider feel comfortable or secure. The panels are often made of felt, covered in leather so that they sit closely to the back. Unlike the other types of saddle mentioned, they are plain, and lacking in any distracting frills. To show off the shoulder to even greater advantage, the saddle is sometimes placed a little farther back than normal. When this is the case, an extra strap, known as a 'point strap' is added so that the girth can be moved forward on the saddle, so that it fits comfortably into the sternum curve. This stops the saddle from slipping forward, and the idea can be successfully employed on ponies with poor conformation on whom any type of saddle tends to slide forward.

Small, fat ponies can often be difficult to fit successfully with leather saddles, and sometimes a felt pad used instead can be the answer to the problem. This is made of thick felt, with leather covering the areas likely to be worn by the stirrup leathers. Fittings are provided for the leathers, whilst the girth is stitched on. Sometimes a leather loop forming a handle is stitched onto the front of the saddle, which can be a reassuring handhold for a small child. The felt pad, having no tree, has no fitting problems, and is also much cheaper to buy than the leather sort. This is perhaps a factor to consider if buying a saddle for a small child who is less likely to care properly for the more expensive item.

Fitting

Whatever type of saddle is bought, it must fit both horse and rider correctly. What is comfortable for one may not be right for the other, and will affect the way the horse goes.

The saddle should be fitted without a numnah in order to make an accurate assessment of its fit on the horse or pony. It should also be girthed up, as this can influence the way it sits. That consideration aside, if the saddle is left without a girth on a horse which moves suddenly, there is a danger of its falling off and being damaged. The saddle should be placed well forwards, and slipped backwards so that the front sits comfortably into the hollow of muscle just behind the shoulder. This ensures that all the hairs of the coat are lying flat and in the same direction.

When selecting a saddle initially, choose one which looks as though it will accommodate both the horse and rider and be suitable for the activities the rider wants to pursue. Once the saddle is girthed up, an initial assessment can be made of it. When looked at from the side, it should appear to sit level on the back, and not be higher at one end than the other. A hand should be slid between the panels and the back, to ensure that they are sitting on the muscle along the length of the panel; it is not uncommon to find that there is a hollow in the region of the waist. This will mean that the rider's weight will form pressure points and possibly sores under the pommel and cantle. From the front, daylight should be clearly visible when looking down through the front arch and along the channel. The saddle should not pinch the backbone, but sit on the muscle on either side, nor should it be so wide that the front of the saddle sits down upon the withers.

The rider should next be mounted in the saddle, and the clearance of the withers checked when weight is present. This should be at least three fingers' breadth between the withers and the front arch.

After about six months, the flocking will settle, and the saddle needs to be restuffed, or else it is likely to rub against the withers. It should be checked again another six months after that, and once a year subsequently.

The saddle should be observed in walk, trot, and canter, since once a rider is mounted and the horse is moving, problems may be spotted which were not obvious before.

13

ACCESSORIES TO THE SADDLE

Numnahs, saddlecloths, and witherpads.
Numnahs should never be used to try to make a badly fitting saddle sit better on a horse or pony; the saddle should either be exchanged or reflocked, since even with a thick numnah, sores can still be caused. Numnahs come in different materials, ranging from genuine sheepskin, felt, synthetic fleece, and cotton quilting, to foam covered with cotton. Their greatest benefit comes when riding a cold backed horse, which resents the initial contact of leather against its skin. The other major factor in their favour is that they protect the saddle lining from damage by dirt and sweat, although they should not be used to save the owner cleaning and soaping the saddle thoroughly! Many people find numnahs useful when bringing an unfit animal back into work again, as a thick one provides some cushioning against the leather, and may prevent sores.

The shape of the numnah should be selected according to the type of saddle it is going to be used with, as well as its size. Sizes available are pony, cob, and full size, whilst the cut may vary, depending on whether it is intended for a straight cut dressage saddle, or a more forward cut jumping saddle.

Saddlecloths have no real function except for what they may add to appearance, and to protect the saddle lining.

Knitted witherpads can be used underneath the front arch of the saddle as a very temporary means of stopping it from rubbing on the withers. This is only temporary, and not a long term solution; the saddle should be changed or adjusted by a saddler at the first possible opportunity.

None of the above should be used in showclasses, although they are frequently seen in other branches of equitation.

Fitting

The most crucial point to make about fitting a numnah, saddlecloth, or witherpad, is that it must be pulled well up into the front arch of the saddle, so that it does not rub the withers. When using a thick numnah, check that it does not drastically alter the fit of the saddle, making the channel too narrow, so that the backbone becomes pinched. The girth straps should be slipped through any tapes supplied, and the girth threaded through the keepers often present at the bottom of the numnah – this is simply a precaution to try and ensure that it does not slip backwards.

Girth sleeves

These are made from tubes of real or synthetic sheepskin, which are slid over the girth itself. They are used on animals which are in soft condition, so that galling is less likely to occur from the unaccustomed contact of a girth, and also on horses and ponies which are prone to galling for some reason.

In the event of a gall ever happening, the cause should always be sought, rather than immediately resorting to a sleeve since, if the problem is due to bad stable management, it can be prevented, and there is no reason why it should ever occur again.

Buckle guards

These are oblong pieces of leather with either two or three slits cut into the top edge, as shown in fig 40. They slip onto the girth straps, and lie over the buckles of the girth, so that damage is not caused to the saddle flaps. Sometimes these or a larger flap are provided with a new saddle; if not, they are a worthwhile and relatively cheap investment, since a new saddle flap is expensive, or a patch unsightly. The larger flap type of guard is often more effective than the smaller ones, and can be stitched to the girth strap webbs so that it does not get lost. Whatever the type, they should always be positioned over the girth buckles after any adjustments have been made. They are not necessary on saddles possessing long girth straps, where a shorter girth not coming into contact with the flaps is used.

40 Buckle guards

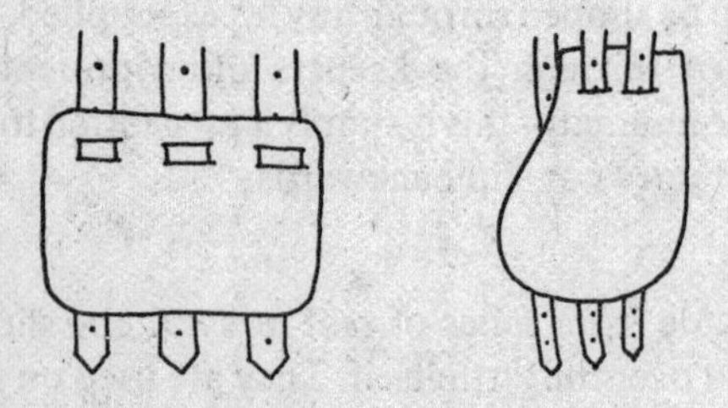

Cruppers

Cruppers are made from leather, attaching to a 'D' ring fitted to the back of the saddle, and looping around the tail, under the dock. Their purpose is to keep the saddle from slipping forwards, most usually on ponies with poor conformation such as straight narrow shoulders. A buckle halfway down the main section allows room for adjustment to the length, whilst a second buckle allows the section passing around the tail to be undone when putting it on and taking it off.

Fitting

The main section of the crupper is threaded through the 'D'

ring at the back of the saddle (sometimes it is necessary to have one of these fitted), and it is adjusted to the correct length. The tail section is then passed under the dock, and buckled up. The tension should be firm, but not so tight that it pulls the tail up or causes discomfort. The dock section should be made of soft, supple leather, and will need regular oiling if the dock is not to become sore.

Stirrup leathers

The most commonly obtainable leathers are made from oak bark tanned cowhide, rawhide or buffalo hide. The last is almost unbreakable, but it does stretch quite considerably. The strength of buffalo hide makes it rather popular in showjumping circles since a great deal of the rider's weight is supported upon the leathers and the irons. Cowhide leathers are made up with the rough, or 'flesh' side facing outwards, unlike other items of saddlery. This is because the smooth, or 'grain' side of the leather is better able to withstand the wear and tear caused by the friction of a stirrup moving against it.

They come in a variety of lengths and widths, so can be selected according to the rider's requirements. Longer leathers can be bought for dressage, when the rider sits with a longer leg. Shorter and narrower leathers can be bought for a small child. It is not ideal to have over-long leathers, since it will mean that a surplus length is left hanging down by the horse or pony's side, which could possibly frighten it. If leathers are not short enough, they can have extra holes punched; they should not be twisted around the iron, as this will damage them. Neither should the rider's foot be placed through the leather instead of through the iron, in order to save on time adjusting them. This could be extremely dangerous should the rider fall off, as the foot is likely to become trapped. However, stirrup leathers which are very slightly longer than required can have advantages; when having them restitched, they can also be slightly shortened.

This means that the stirrup irons will lie in a different part of the leathers, and so they are less likely to wear through too quickly. New leathers will stretch to a certain extent, and unless the rider sits absolutely straight, they will also stretch unevenly. As most riders sit more crooked than they realise, the leathers should be changed to opposite sides of the saddle regularly – say once a week. This helps to keep the lengths as equal as possible.

Stitching should always be checked since it wears fairly quickly, and signs of excessive wear at the points where the iron rests should be noted. Good quality leathers will have three lines of stitching fastening the buckle on.

Seatsavers

These are made of real or acrylic fleece, and are not so much for the good of the saddle as for the rider's seat. They provide a warm and comfortable seat in the colder months of the year, and if the saddle is particularly hard and uncomfortable, make riding less painful. They cover the whole of the seat of the saddle.

14

GIRTHS

The most important thing about a girth is that it must serve its purpose effectively. It must hold the saddle in place on the back. Some girths are working girths, designed for safe everyday use and which can undergo all normal stresses. However, a few, used for showing or dressage, tend to be suitable only for those purposes.

Selecting and fitting a girth

The right length should always be chosen, since too long a girth tends to sit uncomfortably beneath the rider's thighs, and it is dangerous, whilst too short a girth can damage the flaps and panels of the saddle, and pinch the horse or pony's skin. There should always be room for further adjustment to be made once the rider is mounted. This will almost always be necessary, since a rider's weight in the saddle presses it down on the back, making the girth somewhat looser. The ideal height for the girth, once completely tightened, is approximately halfway up the girth straps on both sides. It should also be the same height on both sides if possible, to prevent the saddle from slipping over to one side. The girth buckles should also be on level holes on the girth straps to prevent pinching.

Before mounting, both forelegs should be stretched forwards, so that any wrinkled skin beneath the girth, which could lead to painful pinching and chafing, is straightened out. Once mounted, it should just be possible to insert three fingers firmly between the girth and the skin; care should be taken to slide the fingers smoothly out after checking, so that the hair lies comfortably.

Where there is a choice of girth straps, the girth should be attached to either the first and second, or first and third straps, but always to girth straps which are on separate pieces of webb. This is a safety precaution – in the event of one webb breaking, the other should hold firm. Whatever the arrangement of attaching the girth, it should be the same on both sides.

Three fold leather girth

This girth, as the name implies, is made entirely of a single broad strip of leather, which has been folded over lengthways twice. There are two buckles on each end, for attachment to the girth straps. This girth can be extremely strong and long lasting if it is properly cared for. Keep it as supple as possible to eliminate rubbing. It will need a lot of nourishment as it covers a region of the horse's body which sweats a lot and so dries out the fat content of the leather. The most effective way of coping with this is by inserting a strip of material which has been soaked in neatsfoot oil into the centre of the folds. It works effectively because the warmth of the horse or pony, when it is working, draws the oil through the leather itself, from the very centre. The material should be oiled again from time to time, depending upon the amount of use the girth gets.

When in place, the rounded edge should face forwards to the elbows, so that it does not catch.

The major drawback with this type of girth is the large amount of leather required to make it up, which makes it very expensive to buy, although, properly treated, it should have a long life.

Atherstone girth

At first glance, this appears very similar to the three fold leather girth. It differs however in that it is only a double, rather than treble thickness of leather, and is tapered at the points where it passes behind the elbows. This should avert chafing in the elbow region. As it is completely stitched up into a flattened tube, it is impossible to oil the girth from the inside. Traditionally, an oiled strip of material should be inserted into the centre before it is sewn up.

A variation on this pattern is the Atherstone stretch girth, which incorporates a piece of strong elastic so that the girth can expand with the movement of the horse's ribcage. This makes it a popular jumping girth, although the elastic quickly loses its strength and stretchiness, making replacement of the insert necessary. It should always be used with a breastplate to help maintain the position of the saddle.

Balding girth

This girth follows the same principle as the Atherstone girth in that it tries to minimise the problem of rubbing behind the elbows. It is constructed from a single thickness of leather, divided into three strips. These strips cross over each other, so that the width of the girth is tapered inwards where it passes the elbows.

Nylon string girth

A cheap, durable girth, which is very suitable for small ponies, whose tack is often given rather rougher treatment than that belonging to an adult rider. They are easy to clean, as they can be washed in a bucket of hot soapy water, and dry quickly afterwards. The strings allow for better circulation of air, which can help to reduce the possibility of galling due to excessive sweating. Adults tightening these girths for younger children should be careful not to fasten them too tightly on a small pony.

If a string, or strings, become broken, the girth should be replaced, otherwise nasty pinches can arise.

41 Various types of girth

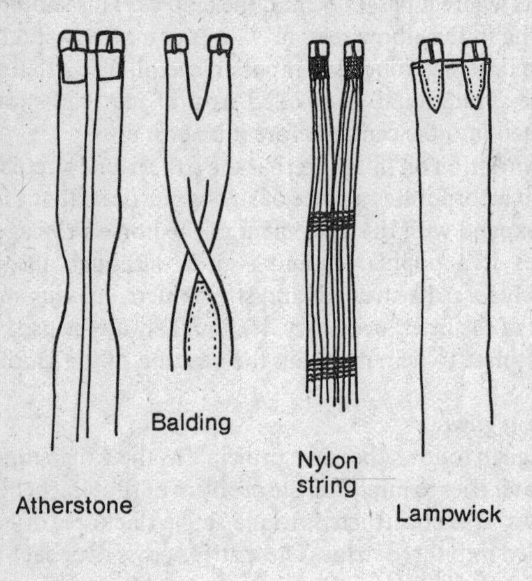

Lampwick girth

Lampwick can look very smart when new or recently washed, but does not always make an ideal material for a girth. Being very soft, it has its uses on horses and ponies which are very unfit, or prone to galling easily, but since it is made from cotton and wool tubular webb, it rots very quickly, stretches considerably, and frays, often breaking with little or no warning. The moment any fraying is noticed, for the sake of safety, a new girth should be bought.

Lampwick girths can be washed in hot soapy water, but the leather attaching the buckles to the girth should be well oiled before and afterwards, and protected by Vaseline whilst being washed. Check carefully for any cracking in the leather.

Synthetic and cotton mix girths

These are a more modern and practical alternative to lampwick girths. They are very soft whilst still being strong, easy to clean, long lasting and ideal for horses and ponies prone to galling. Although not suitable for showing they are good, working girths which are not over-expensive to buy.

Buffalo hide girths

These are cheap leather girths, usually of single thickness, and easily identified by a rather greasy feel, and reddish colour. They stretch considerably, and are usually of cheap workmanship – buckles are often attached to leather which has been glued down, rather than stitched. Another disadvantage is that they can chafe behind the elbows.

Dressage girths

There are two variations of girth designed for use with dressage saddles possessing long girth straps. Both are shorter than a normal girth, the idea being that without any buckles beneath the saddle flaps, the rider's legs can come into closer contact with the horse's sides. One girth has just two buckles at each end, whilst the other variation has an additional leather strap with an elastic insert, running down the centre as shown in fig 42. A buckle is stitched onto both ends of this strap, and fastens to a strap situated at the bottom of the saddle flaps, so that they do not ride upwards beneath the rider's leg.

A problem with these types of girth lies in the extra length of girth strap necessary; since they are so long, greater strain is imposed upon them and they are more liable to break. This should not affect their use when working on the flat, but a dressage saddle with long girth straps is not advisable for

42 A dressage girth

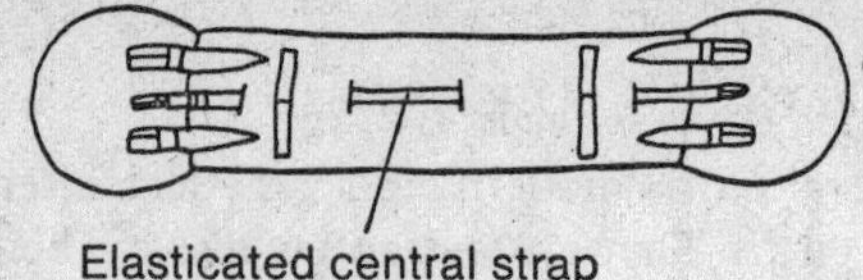

more strenuous activities.

Some horses do not accept such girths kindly, as clumsy tightening of the girth can pinch the skin, leading to bad temper. When mounted, it is advisable to have a second person available to tighten the girth further. It is difficult to do so from on board, and possibly also dangerous if the horse is excitable.

Showing girths

Showing girths are made of two pieces of tubular cotton joined together in the centre where they pass beneath the belly. This section sometimes also has a piece of pimpled rubber covering it, which gives better grip to stop the saddle slipping.

This type of girth helps to exhibit a horse or pony to better effect. It is very perishable though, and, since it is not as strong and reliable as a working girth, should be both carefully maintained and kept only for use in the show ring. Discomfort can be caused if it is overtightened.

Webb girths

Girths made from cotton, wool, or cotton/wool mixture only have one buckle on each end, and so should be used in pairs for safety. They are notorious for breaking unexpectedly. Having two girths reduces the risk of mishap. They also need to be kept scrupulously clean to prevent rubbing.

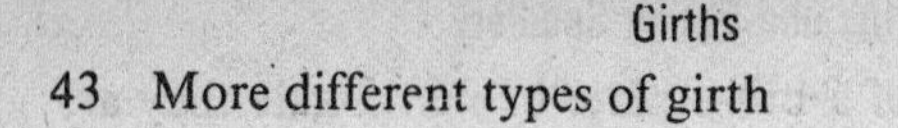

43 More different types of girth

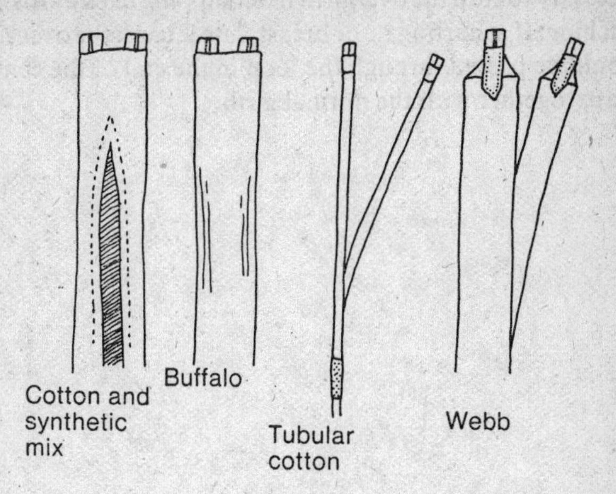

Overgirth

An overgirth differs from the others in that it is used as an additional means of securing a saddle, not as a substitute for a normal girth. Whenever a horse or pony jumps, its ribcage expands considerably, and could snap a girth, or the webb attaching a girth strap to the saddle. The overgirth, which should ideally have an elastic insert so that it can expand with the ribcage, should avert a bad accident in such an event.

The overgirth is made from a piece of webb, elasticated and with a narrow leather strap at one end, and a buckle and keeper at the other. It passes over the top of the saddle and girth, and should be buckled up tightly beneath the belly by an assistant on the ground. If loops are provided on the saddle flaps for the purpose, the overgirth can be slipped through these. The position of the keepers may need changing by a saddler, as they often are not in the right place, but in the absence of a breastplate or martingale they are necessary to stop the overgirth from slipping backwards and pinching. If a martingale or breastplate is used, the overgirth should be passed through the loop in the end of the central strap, together with the normal girth.

15

PROTECTIVE SADDLERY AND CLOTHING

'Protective' saddlery consists not just of clothing to protect against injury whilst travelling, but also whilst working. There is much variation in the materials used, particularly for working boots, where modern synthetic materials now play a large part – but the basic traditional patterns remain the same. The important factor when choosing a working boot is that the material is suitable for the purpose for which it is intended. A felt brushing boot, for example would not be very practical for jumping across country through mud and water, whereas a synthetic boot would be tougher, withstanding the rigours of such treatment, and easier to clean.

Travelling Equipment

Travelling boots

These are rapidly gaining popularity as a quick and easy way of providing protection when travelling, since they are less time-consuming to put on, and more convenient than bandages if a horse or pony is likely to be excitable at a show. Another big advantage is that it is impossible to injure a horse or pony putting them on, whilst a badly applied bandage can damage the tendons.

They are usually made of vinyl with a felt or acrylic fleece lining. The fastenings are generally clips, or wide strips of velcro which should be kept brushed clean so that they fasten properly. See fig 45 on page 125.

Fitting
These boots should reach from the knee to hock to the coronary band. The back boots should be slightly longer to allow for the extra length of the cannon bone. You must ensure that the boots cover the lower region of the leg, so that adequate protection is given to that part of the limb most likely to sustain damage.

Knee boots
These are made from a combination of rugging and leather, designed to give protection to the knees should the horse fall during travelling. The rugging is edged with a contrasting binding, so that the boots can be colour co-ordinated with rugs for a smart turn out at shows.

Fitting
The top strap is fastened so that the buckle faces to the outside, not the inside, of the leg. It should be soft and supple, so that chafing does not occur, and needs to be buckled firmly above the knee joint although it should not restrict the circulation. There should be room to admit one finger. The lower strap should never be done up so tightly as to impede flexion of the joint, nor left so loose as to allow the possibility of a foot becoming entangled in it. About a palm's breadth admitted between the lower strap and the leg should be adequate. When removing, the lower strap should be unbuckled first, so that the boot does not fall around the feet. See fig 44.

44 Knee boot and hock boot

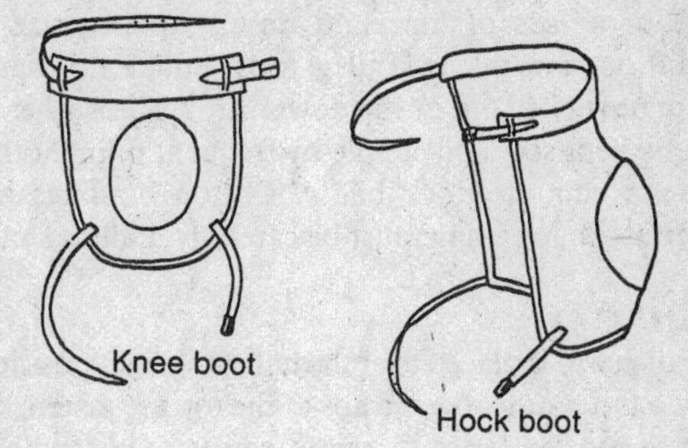

Hock boots

Similarly to knee boots, these are made of rugging and leather, designed to protect the hock if the horse falls down whilst travelling, or if it kicks out at the partitions. As with knee boots, the colour of rugging and binding can be selected to co-ordinate with travelling rugs.

Fitting

The top strap is fastened so that the buckle is facing to the outside of the leg, not the inside. This strap should be soft and supple also, so that no rubbing occurs. It should be fastened fairly firmly, so that it admits one finger at the front of the hock. See fig 44. The lower strap should admit a palm's breadth, and not be fastened too tightly or loosely, for the reasons mentioned above under KNEE BOOTS.

Tail guard

These are made of leather or jute or of rugging with a contrasting binding, and can be used either on top of, or instead of, a tail bandage, to give protection to the tail whilst travelling. Some horses and ponies will rub their tails on partitions, or brace themselves against the ramp, which can result in a loss of hair and untidy appearance, unless precautions are taken. Tail guards, unlike tail bandages, cannot be rubbed off, or slip downwards. The leather variety must be kept soft and supple by frequent oiling, otherwise they can rub the dock badly. Cotton bindings are not colourfast, so cleaning must be carefully undertaken.

Fittings

The tail guard is placed over the tail in the right position, and the two tapes or leather straps at the top are fastened to the roller. Then the tapes or straps across the breadth of the guard should be fastened securely on the top of the tail, rather than underneath it, where they could irritate. Fastening them in this order prevents any tail hairs from being rubbed up the wrong way and broken if a tail bandage is not used. If tapes are used, rather than leather straps, care must be taken to ensure that they lie flat, and do not cut into the dock, as not only will it cause pain if they do, but loss of circulation to the area leads to the hairs eventually falling out.

Poll guard

Poll guards, as the name implies, protect the poll, or roof of the skull, when travelling. See fig 45. Sometimes there is a danger that a horse, particularly a nervous traveller, or one which is bad to load or unload, will throw up its head. Once it has hurt itself, not only is there the problem of having to treat the injury, but also it is likely to make the animal more difficult to load and travel in the future. Poll guards are generally made of foam, felt, leather, or a combination of any of these. A simple and economical poll guard can be made by obtaining a piece of thick foam rubber, cutting two slits in it, and then threading the headpiece of a headcollar through.

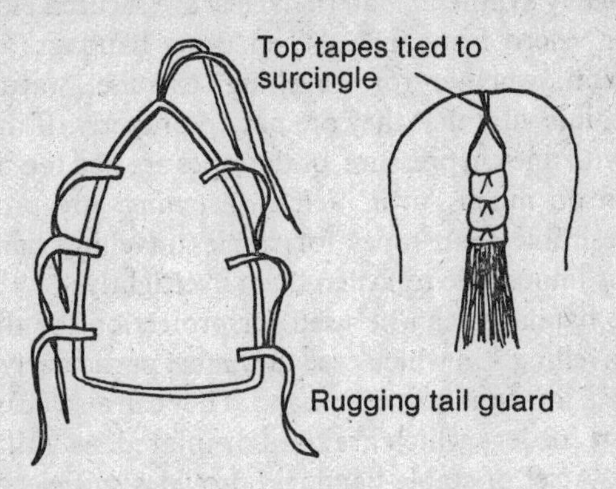

45 (*Above*) A tail guard
(*Below*) A poll guard

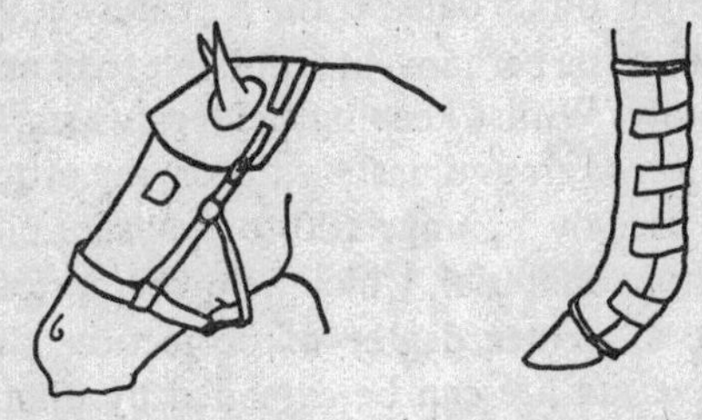

Fitting

The headpiece of the headcollar is slotted through the slits provided; more sophisticated versions also incorporate two holes for the ears, which help it to maintain its position better, and afford greater protection. Care should always be taken when introducing a poll guard for the first time, as a few horses may be scared initially.

Travelling and stable bandages

These are made from wool, a woollen/synthetic mix, or from a completely synthetic material. They are secured either by tapes or velçro fastenings. When using bandages of any description, whether for travelling, exercise, warmth or support, it is vital that they are put on properly. If they are put on with uneven pressure, or the tapes are tied too tightly, they can do much harm. Velcro fastenings are probably more desirable than tapes for stable/travelling bandages since it is impossible to fasten them overtightly.

These bandages can be used for protection for the legs when travelling – in which case they must particularly cover the fetlock joint and coronary band. They can also be used as a support for legs which are tired or injured, as well as for warmth. A set of stable bandages provides sufficient extra warmth to make it possible to use one blanket fewer. This can be preferable for a sick animal which perhaps cannot cope with extra weight on its back. If the legs are wet, cold and muddy – after hunting perhaps – it is possible to bandage over the top of straw. Whilst keeping the legs warm, this allows the circulation of air and hastens the drying process. Normally they are used over gamgee, cotton pads, or pieces of synthetic foam type material, which help keep pressure even, and provide a greater degree of protection. Since gamgee is expensive, its life can be extended by blanket-stitching around the edges with cotton thread to stop it from fraying and falling apart. Horses and ponies should not be turned out in any form of bandage.

Fitting (See fig 46)

Bandages should always be unrolled against the leg, as this helps to keep the pressure even. A piece of gamgee should be placed around the leg first, and the bandage should begin just beneath the knee or hock, following the same direction as the gamgee, otherwise it will become loose and fall off.

46 How to fit stable bandages

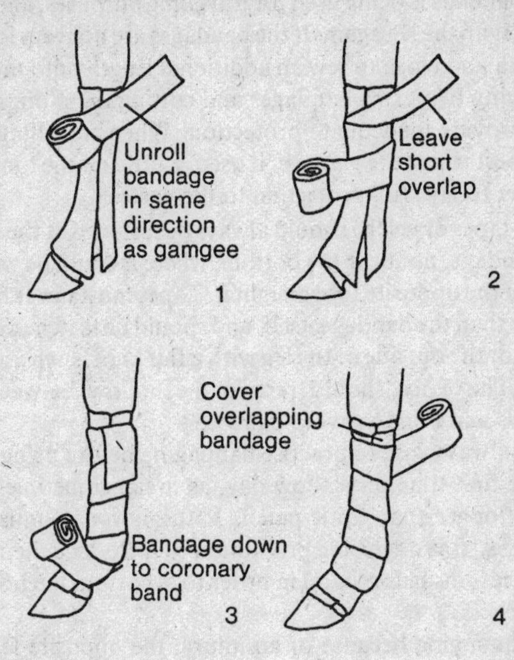

Unroll the bandage against the leg, firmly and at a downwards angle, making sure the pastern is well protected if the bandage is being used for travelling purposes, and then return it up the leg again. If the bandages are not very long, it can be a good idea to sew an additional length onto the end, by buying two extra bandages and cutting them up, rather than provide inadequate protection. When travelling, it is often best to cut the gamgee, if used, a little on the long side in order to give full protection to the pastern.

The tapes or velcro should always be fastened at the top of the bandage, not near the bottom, where it could be worked loose if the opposite foot caught it. Tapes must never be tied tighter than the bandage itself, and should be fastened on the inside or the outside of the leg with a flat knot, such as a reef knot. This knot should rest in the hollow between the tendons and bone to avoid damage.

It is always wise to practise bandaging before using them for the first time on a show day, as it can sometimes take rather longer than anticipated. If the horse is unused to bandages, it is a sensible precaution to introduce them on a few occasions beforehand in order to accustom the horse to their feel.

If bandaging because of an injury, the opposite leg will also require a bandage, since it is likely to be taking the strain from the affected leg, and needs to be supported. On removing the bandages, shavings and straw should be brushed off so that the bandages are ready for use next time, and they should be rolled with the tapes or velcro to the inside.

Tail bandage

Exercise bandages can be used as tail bandages, provided they have tapes, rather than hook fastenings. They protect the tail from damage during a journey, and keep its appearance neat and tidy, particularly if it is a pulled tail. They can be used as well as, or instead of, a tail guard.

Fitting

Lift the tail, and pass one end of the rolled bandage beneath the dock, leaving a short length to turn over at the top. After one or two loops around the top of the tail, fold the extra length downwards, and continue bandaging in a downwards direction until the end of the tail bone is reached. Pressure must be firm and even, as a tight loop could lead to loss of circulation and hair. A knot or bow can be tied at the bottom of the bandage – it should not be doubled back up the tail and tied at the top, or halfway down, the dock. (If this is done, and the horse does rub its tail, the knot is likely to come undone, or pressure will be placed on the bone.) If the bandage is being used to tidy up the appearance of a tail, the hairs can be dampened a little first, but the bandage itself must never be made wet, as it could shrink. Tail bandages should not be left on for more than a few hours.

Sausage boot

This boot consists of a large stuffed leather ring, which is fitted around the coronet to prevent injury to the elbow when a horse or pony is stabled. Some animals have a tendency to injure themselves when lying down, by catching the elbow with the heel of a shoe, so that an unsightly enlargement eventually forms.

Fitting

The boot should be buckled around the coronet so that it is a snug fit.

Working Equipment

Exercise bandages

These are used as a substitute for brushing boots, and to provide additional support for the tendons. They are not ideal if working in very wet conditions as the fabric can shrink, and become very waterlogged. Their advantage over boots is that less dirt works its way down between them and the legs, and so the skin is less likely to become sore. Made of elasticated crêpe, they are very stretchy at first, but after several uses, soon lose this quality and should be replaced. Even more care needs to be taken in putting them on than with stable bandages, because their very stretchiness makes it all too easy to apply uneven pressure. Fastenings are either non-stretch tapes, or elastic with hook fastenings.

Fitting (See fig 47)
The bandages should be used over a piece of gamgee cut to a suitable length, or some such synthetic material. This helps to keep pressure even around the leg, and also gives a greater degree of protection against a blow to the leg. They should reach from just beneath the knee or hock joints to the fetlock, without impairing movement in these areas. Unroll the bandage at a downwards angle, bandaging with the gamgee. Pressure must be kept even, but fairly tight. Return the bandage up the leg again, and secure the tapes at the top with the hook fastenings or a knot, to the outside of the leg. It is important that the knot lies between bone and tendon, if non-stretch tapes are used. Exercise bandages must be fastened on the outside of the legs, since otherwise if brushing occurs, the tapes could easily become undone. Tapes should further be secured by taping over the top with surgical or insulating tape, or alternatively by stitching them in place.

Knee caps
These are made of leather, or a combination of leather and rugging, but differ slightly in their design from the knee boots used for travelling. They are used when hacking, especially on roads, or stony surfaces, since falling or stumbling could scar the knees, or cause a more serious injury. Fast work, or jumping, should not be considered

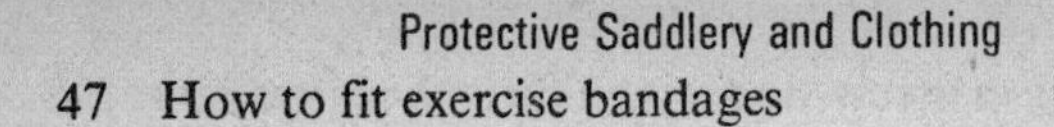

47 How to fit exercise bandages

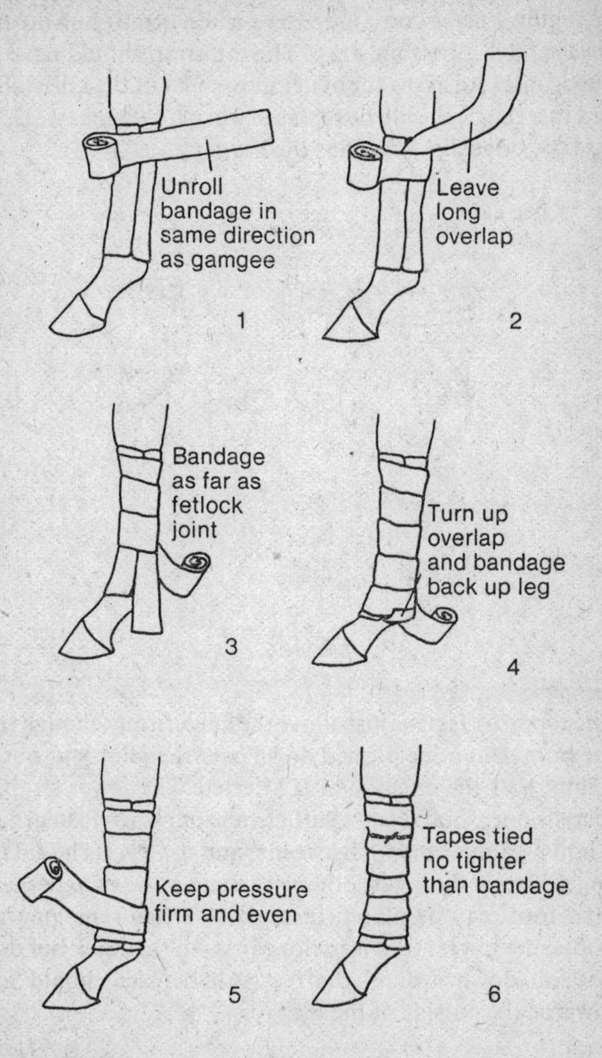

when working in them – and it is unlikely that anyone would consider doing such work on bad going anyway. Like travelling knee boots, they have a top strap, but do not always have a bottom strap. The top strap should have an elastic insert to allow for better movement of the knee joint, and this elastic should be replaced when it becomes weak, in case the boot slips and trips the horse up.

48 Knee caps

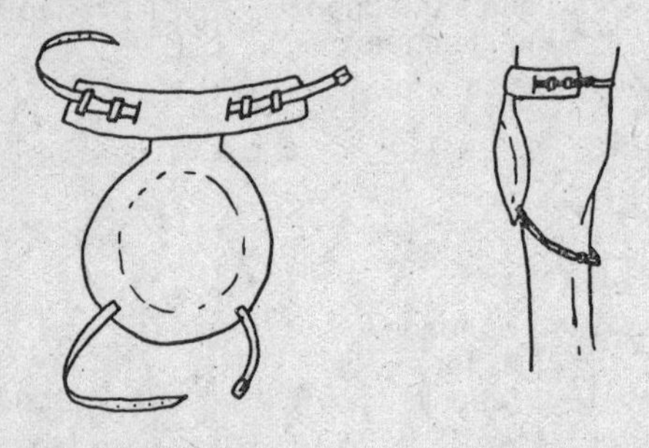

Fitting

The top strap fastens just above the knee, firmly enough that the boot cannot be pushed down over the joint, but not so tightly that the circulation is affected. The lower strap, if there is one, should leave sufficient room when fastened, to admit a palm's breadth between it and the leg. It should not be left looser than this, otherwise there is the danger that a hind foot may be placed through it. When removing the boots, the lower strap is undone first, so that the boot does not fall down around the feet. All buckles should face towards the outside of the leg.

Overreach Boots

Overreach boots are cup shaped pieces of rubber which are placed over the hooves of the front feet, as shown in fig 49, in order to protect the heel region from damage caused by the toes of the back feet. This is most likely to happen when riding a horse which is over active behind, young and unbalanced, or when riding at speed through deep going. They are either all in one piece, or split down one side, with leather or plastic laces to fasten them. Velcro tapes can also be used, but prove somewhat less satisfactory since, when they become dirty, the tapes do not fasten properly, and the boot can become lost. A lacing method makes putting the boots on a lot easier, but the laces tend to pull away from the rubber.

Fitting

The boot should cover the hoof and rear of the heel. One piece boots should first be turned inside out, and pulled on – Vaseline smeared around the edges makes this a bit easier with new boots, until the rubber has stretched a bit. Alternatively, placing them in hot water for a few minutes makes them more elastic and easier to put on, but is not always practical. Overreach boots can sometimes rub the back of the pastern if the horse or pony is unused to wearing them, so they should only be used for short periods initially. A little Vaseline around the tops will help to stop rubbing as well.

Anti-brushing ring

This is a hollow rubber ring placed around the coronet, to shield the area from damage by brushing, when a foot moves too closely to the opposite one. A leather or nylon strap runs inside the rubber ring, which is split at one point so that it can be fitted around the coronet, as shown in fig 49.

49 Anti-brushing ring, overreach boots and fetlock boots

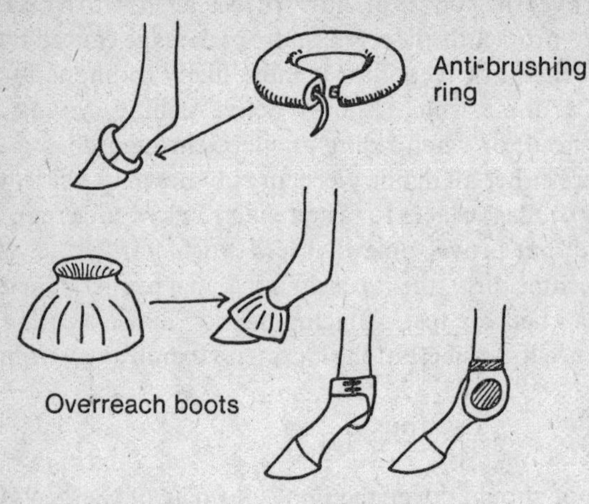

Fitting

The ring is placed around the coronet, and the strap running inside buckled, so that it is a close but not tight fit.

Brushing boots

Brushing boots protect the rear and inside of the lower legs from damage by the other feet when working. They also give protection to the front of the legs when jumping. They are made from leather, felt, or a combination of the two, or from plastic or vinyl. Leather and plastic boots are sometimes lined with rubber, which tends to make the legs very sweaty, although it is easy to clean. If leather boots are left unlined, an eye should be kept on the legs, as the stitching on the inside can rub badly if the horse or pony has sensitive skin. Soft synthetic linings are frequently seen nowadays, which absorb sweat, as well as impact. When selecting brushing boots, decide carefully upon the material they are made of. Leather needs good care and maintenance, but is soft and durable. Plastics are easy to keep clean, and so come into their own for everyday use, when absorbent boots would not be practical; plastics will not absorb the moisture. However, they do have a shorter life, becoming brittle and falling apart, and are not usually repairable. Felt is very soft and comfortable, but not practical for use in wet and muddy conditions – it also wears quickly if there is no leather on the inside of the leg, or if the horse brushes badly. It also rots easily.

50 Brushing boots

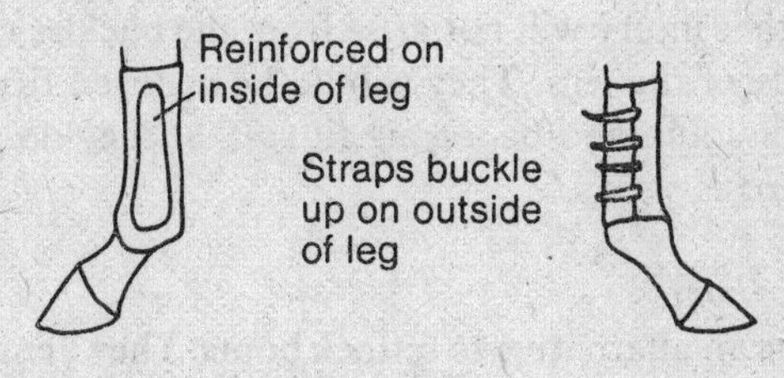

Brushing boots have either three, four, or five straps. Three or four strap boots should be used on the front legs, four or five strap boots on the back legs, since the cannon bone is longer. It is best to refrain from using boots with velcro straps for jumping or cross country, when an accident could happen if they come undone.

Fitting

All boots should be fitted so that the buckles or fastenings face the outside, where they cannot damage the other legs, with the ends of the straps facing backwards. They should be positioned so that they cover the fetlock joint adequately, and not be placed too high. Fasten them so that they are a snug, firm fit. There should be no gap where the two edges of the boot meet. If the animal wearing them has large wind-galls around the fetlock area, it is sometimes necessary to do the bottom strap up much less tightly than the others in order to allow the fetlock joint to move comfortably.

Fetlock boot (fig 49 page 134)
If a horse or pony brushes or knocks itself with its feet in the fetlock region only, fetlock boots can be used instead of brushing boots. Made of leather, or leather and felt, they are fastened just above the fetlock joint by one or two straps.

Fitting
The buckle or buckles should face the outside of the leg, so that further injury will not arise from the buckles catching the inside of the legs. They should be fastened firmly just above the joint, and be a snug fit so that they do not slip downwards.

Yorkshire boots
These are an alternative to fetlock boots. They are made of oblong pieces of kerseycloth, which is a felted wool which is strong and durable and does not fray. A tape is stitched across the middle.

Fitting (see fig 51)
The boot is held around the fetlock joint, and the tapes doubled around just above the joint and tied with a reef knot, so that the knot lies between tendon and bone to the outside of the leg. The longer half of the material should face upwards, so that once the tapes have been tied, it can be flapped downwards, giving more cushioning against a blow from the opposite hoof than just a single thickness would. There should be just enough room for one finger to be

inserted between the boot and leg. Sometimes velcro is used instead of tape; the former is somewhat quicker to fasten.

51 How to fit Yorkshire boots

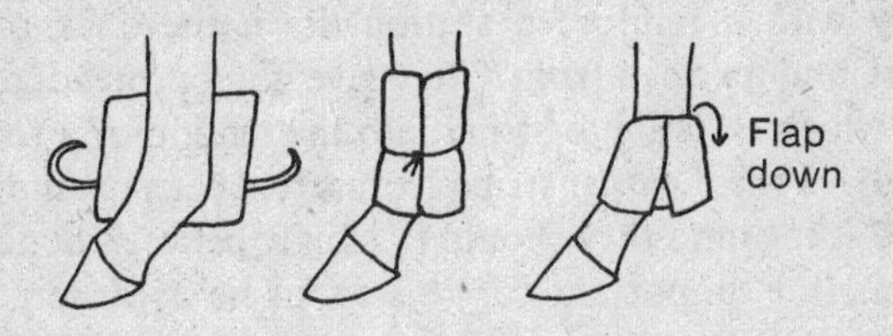

Polo boots

Polo boots, made from felt or a combination of felt and leather, give more extensive protection than brushing boots, since they cover the entire fetlock joint, as shown in fig 52.

52 Front and back polo boots

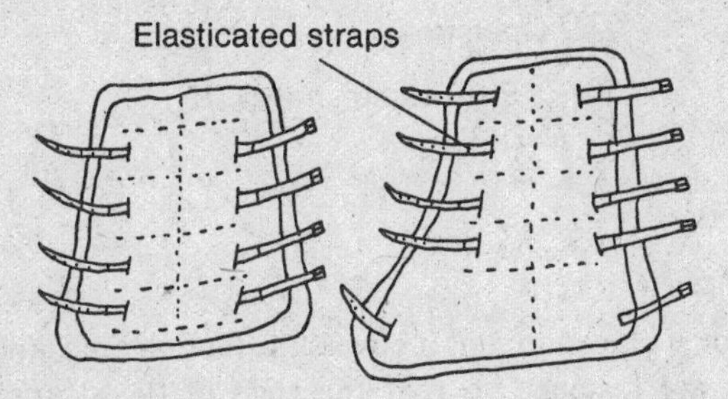

Fitting

All buckles fasten on the outside of the leg, and as with a normal brushing boot, are fastened firmly. Sometimes there is an additional strap which buckles around the pastern; this should be done up loosely, so that movement is not restricted in the fetlock joint.

Tendon boots

These are designed especially to give support to weak tendons, or tendons which are liable to be undergoing great stress, such as when jumping large fences, or working in heavy going. They are made from either leather or plastic, usually with a reinforced section down the back of the tendon, and an open front. They give good protection to a horse which is liable to strike into the tendon of a foreleg with a back toe. Leather strips are inserted between the boot and its lining, and they should fit snugly between bone and tendon. It is important for this fit to be as accurate as possible. 'Off the peg' boots may not be suitable and may place pressure on the tendons instead of supporting them. The straps fastening the boots should be elasticated, since to do any good they must not only fit properly, but also be fairly tight. See fig 53.

53 Tendon boots

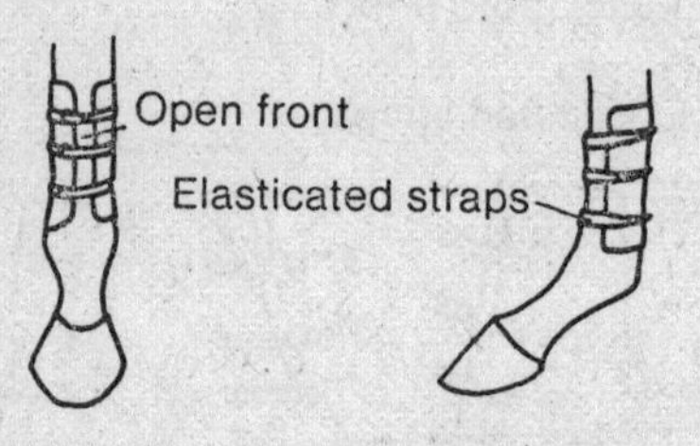

Fitting

The boot is placed so that it covers the tendon area, and the buckles are fastened so that the ends of the straps face towards the outside of the legs. It should be possible to insert one finger tightly between the boot and the leg.

On removing any boots or bandages, it is a good idea to massage the legs with the hands in order to restore proper circulation.

16

RUGS

The purposes of rugs can be many; to keep a horse or pony warm, protect it from the weather, keep it clean, assist in air circulation to help it dry off when wet. There are so many different brand names on the market now, that it is impossible to include them all in this chapter, especially since new variations are being produced all the time. Therefore this chapter concentrates on conventional rugs and materials – the principles of fitting remain basically the same after all. Information concerning a new product can always be sought from the manufacturer.

Rugs are bought in different sizes, ranging from about 4′6″ upwards to 6′6″ or 7′, in 3″ steps. This measurement refers to the length of the rug, the distance usually being taken from the middle of the chest to the back of the rug. The measurement should be checked with a tape measure when buying. Rugs also vary considerably in both the quality of materials used – the heavier the fabric the more durable it is likely to be – and also in the cut. Heavier duty rugs will always cost more initially, but may save expense later in repairs and replacements. Similarly, rugs which have been shaped so that they fit the horse more comfortably, and which are deeper through the girth, will also cost more. Do not grudge the extra expense. It does at least ensure peace of mind to know that the animal is more likely to keep them in place without causing sore and rubbed patches.

Jute/flax and nylon quilted rugs

These are used as stable rugs, either when it is cold, to provide extra warmth, or when a horse or pony has been clipped, to replace the lost coat. Jute and flax rugs are perishable, but if promptly repaired when damaged, and cleaned and stored properly each spring, they can be surprisingly durable, with a lifespan of at least five years. They are either fully, or half-lined with a woollen or woollen/synthetic mixture blanket so that they are both warmer and more comfortable. If the weather is particularly harsh, and the horse or pony is feeling the cold, additional blankets can be added separately beneath the rug. If the animal was already wearing a jute or flax rug before being clipped, then at least one or more extra blankets should be added after clipping.

The rugs are fastened at the chest by one or two breast straps made of leather or nylon webb, with a plastic or steel buckle.

Nylon quilted rugs are not perishable as the natural fibre ones are, but can be prone to snags and tears. Some rugs are designed as an all-in-one rug, where no additional blankets should be necessary, but with the thinner quilted type, they most usually are. Quilted rugs have an advantage over natural fibre in that they are usually easy to wash in a washing machine, and they do have a smart appearance when clean, so that they could serve as a show rug as well. Cotton-lined, rather than nylon-lined versions appear to be more successful as they are less likely to make a horse or pony sweat, and they do not slip quite as much. The biggest drawback with quilted rugs is the difficulty encountered when rugging up a hot or sweating horse, or one prone to 'breaking out' after exercise, as they keep the animal too warm, and do not allow for much circulation of air or absorption of moisture.

New Zealand rugs (fig 54)
New Zealand rugs are available in different weights of canvas, flax, or nylon, and are used to turn a horse or pony out in cold weather. Many native breeds are hardy enough to cope with most bad weather, but finer types, and those which are clipped do need extra protection against the elements. As with stable rugs, the heavier the weight of the fabric, the tougher it will be, and this is important when considering the amount of wear and tear it will have to take whilst out in the field. Prompt maintenance ensures a longer life, as will reproofing to keep it waterproof. Tins of wax for this purpose can be bought from good saddlers.

54 A New Zealand rug

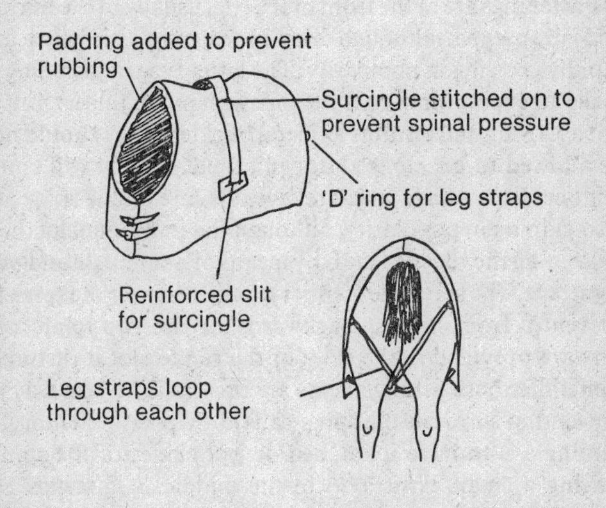

New Zealand rugs usually have half, rather than full blanket linings for warmth. This is for purely practical reasons, as a full lining would quickly become muddy and waterlogged.

If the rug is needed on an everyday basis, and particularly if the horse or pony is living out all the time, it is a good idea to purchase two, rather than just one, if the expense can be met. This makes it possible to have repairs dealt with when they arise, since a spare rug is available, and in particularly bad weather, they can be alternated so that each has a chance to dry out. In any case, a rug which is worn all the time should be removed, checks made for sores, and then replaced straight, at least once or twice a day.

Additional protection can be given by buying a hood for the head – this can be bought separately from the rug if desired. They not only will keep a horse or pony that little bit warmer, but are very useful with the sort which gets excessively muddy.

Fastenings are at the front of the rug, usually of the buckle and strap type, although easy-to-fasten plastic clips are rapidly growing in popularity. The latter type of fastening is easier to cope with in cold weather with numb fingers, but is not as strong and durable as metal buckles. They should not be allowed to get clogged up with mud, or they will come undone. Belly straps which relieve pressure on the spine are also gaining in popularity, although the traditional method of keeping the rug in place is by means of a surcingle and two leg straps. The surcingle is either stitched on over the spine to prevent it from slipping backwards, or else two reinforced slits are provided in the sides of the rug to slot it through; sometimes both arrangements are present. The best way of preventing sores on the spine caused by pressure from the surcingle is to have it stitched on both sides of the spine, leaving a small extra loop in the middle. Leg straps are manufactured from nylon or leather; both should be kept clean, and the leather variety kept as supple as possible. Applications of neatsfoot oil or a similar preparation will do this, as well as protect the leather from damage. Leg straps should be fastened one around each back leg, and linked through each other to minimise any danger of rubbing on the insides of the stifle, and to help keep the rug as straight as possible.

Summer sheets
Summer sheets are made from cotton or linen, and in a selection of different colours which can be selected to harmonise with show equipment. They are useful in the summer to help prevent stable stains, and to keep flies off a stabled horse or pony, whilst still being light enough to enable the animal to stay cool. It is possible to turn horses out in them in order to keep stains to a minimum, although tears and rips must be expected occasionally, as they are not designed to withstand such rough treatment. They are also useful for putting next to the horse's skin during the winter, when other clothing is also being worn, as they will help to keep blankets and the linings of rugs clean; it is much easier to wash a summer sheet than a rug. Some horses and ponies can prove to be allergic to wool or woollen/synthetic mixes, in which instance a summer sheet between the skin and the rug or blanket will reduce any discomfort. When travelling an animal during the summer, it is often too hot to put a day rug or similar on, so a summer sheet could be used instead, both for appearance and to keep draughts off the horse's back during the trip.

Day rugs
Made of wool or a woollen/synthetic mixture, they are put on the horse during the daytime, and are exchanged at night for a more serviceable jute or quilted rug. They are not essential, but rather for appearances. They can be used beneath stable rugs instead of a blanket, but as they are expensive, unless it is an old rug, it seems silly to do so. It should be possible to obtain them in a variety of colours with a contrasting binding, so that they can be matched up with other equipment. Cotton bindings are not colourfast.

Different weights of day rug can be obtained; melton cloth, which is very lightweight, or else 2lb or 3lb rugging. The heavier the weight of wool, the warmer the rug.

Sweat sheets

These are the equivalent of string vests worn by humans, with a similar appearance, and used for wet horses and ponies. Rather than being worn on their own, they should be used beneath another rug, even if it is only a light one, so that pockets of air are caught in the holes of the sheet. Air is allowed to circulate, which helps to evaporate the moisture on the horse, and yet it is still kept warm. This can be particularly important during cold weather as moisture on a horse or pony exposed directly to the air quickly becomes cold, and can lead to chills.

Neck sweaters

These are made of rugging, although it is possible to make a simple version from an old blanket at home. They are most commonly seen on horses or ponies which are used for showing, either to reduce the amount of excess fatty tissue, or for helping to bring summer coats through more quickly for early shows; as the neck is not usually covered by a rug or blanket, it sometimes has a hairier appearance than the rest of the body. Holes are provided for the eyes and ears, and the whole is fastened beneath the jaw and neck by tapes. A further tape is sewn to the base of the sweater so that it can be attached to the roller or surcingle; thus it cannot be rubbed off.

Blankets

As the weather gets colder in the winter, so it is sometimes necessary to add blankets beneath the stable rugs. Last thing at night and first thing in the morning are the best times to check to see if the horse or pony is warm enough, or even too hot, so that blankets can be added or removed as necessary. Feeling the ears is usually a good guide as to the comfort of the animal; if they are cold, the rest of the body usually is too.

It is best to put blankets on at night, and remove one or more during the daytime when the weather is generally milder, otherwise the full benefit is not felt later on at night, when the temperature normally drops. If the weather proves to be unusually harsh, they can of course, be left on all the time.

Rugging up and adding blankets in the late autumn and early winter months, before they are really required, can help to keep the winter coat fairly fine and light. If it is not desirable to clip a horse or pony because it is badly behaved during the process, this can be done, and saves much aggravation. Blankets are generally made of pure wool, (which is warm but heavy and expensive) of a woollen/synthetic mixture, or even wholly synthetic.

Waterproof and exercise sheets

In cold or wet weather, extra protection to keep the horse warm and dry during exercise can be given by using an exercise blanket, or rain sheet. The exercise blanket is similar to a shortened blanket, long enough to cover the quarters and to extend just in front of the saddle, but without a breast fastening. Place the blanket beneath the saddle, making sure that it is pulled well up into the keepers provided for the purpose before tightening it up. It is advisable to attach a fillet string to it, as a sudden gust of wind could blow it upwards and frighten the horse.

A waterproof alternative is made of polyurethane-coated nylon, and can be used on its own, or over the top of a woollen rug. Both these rugs are particularly handy for use on animals which have been extensively clipped, as they are more likely to feel the cold when on slow exercise.

It is possible to buy full-length rain sheets as well as the shorter exercise ones; these are used on top of another rug, often seen at shows. These are usually made of waterproof bri-nylon. When being used to keep the horse and its rugs or saddlery dry, they should be secured by a surcingle, and the use of a fillet string to prevent the back from blowing up.

Some of the waterproof rugs can be rather rustly, and so care should be taken when putting one on for the first time, as a nervous horse can be frightened by it.

Putting on a rug

The easiest way to put on a rug is first to fold it in half, across its length, and to throw it over the horse or pony's back fairly well forward, so that it lies across the withers. The front of the rug has a semi-circular piece cut out of it to fit more snugly around the neck, so check that it is facing in the right direction when using this method. If a New Zealand rug is being put on, the leg straps should not be left dangling, but be fastened to their 'D' rings or eyelets first so that they don't swing around and catch the horse unexpectedly.

The next stage is to unfold the rug gently back over the quarters, and then slide it back a little so that all the hairs lie flat. The roller or surcingle (see ROLLERS AND SURCINGLES) can then be fastened, followed by the buckles on the front of the rug. If leg straps are present they can be detached from their 'D' rings, looped through the legs, and re-attached. Putting a rug on in this manner makes it much easier to get it on straight, with the minimum of fuss, and causing as little harm to the spine as possible. The surcingle or roller must always be fastened first. Should the breast straps be done up first instead, and the horse suddenly moves, there is a danger that the rug will slip and hang around its neck. This could not only cause panic but a torn rug and damage to the neck muscles could follow.

When a blanket is added as shown in fig 55, it should be put on first, doubling it up to half the length and laying it over the quarters, then unfolding it up the neck. The rug is then placed on top, as described above, ensuring that the blanket is not moved in the process. Then the corners of the blanket are flapped up at the front into a triangle and folded back to lie on top of the rug. The roller can then be fastened, followed by the breast straps. This is shown in fig 55. An alternative is to fasten both breast straps and roller, and then roll the blanket back to form a collar; this method helps to keep the chest much warmer.

If it is felt that a blanket is necessary in addition to the New Zealand rug, it is better to stitch it in properly to the existing half lining, rather than to add it separately, otherwise it is likely to slip if the horse rolls.

It is not a wise idea to rug up a sweating or wet horse immediately as the blankets will become soaked, and the horse chilled. Once the horse or pony has been walked around until it is cool, a sweat rug should be placed beneath the stable rug, which should be turned upside down so that the blanket lining does not become soaked. If a sweat rug is not available, the horse or pony can be 'thatched' by placing dry clean straw beneath the reversed stable rug. This will allow the air to circulate, and keep the horse warm. Later, the animal can be brushed off, and the rugs replaced normally.

On warmer days, the front of the rug can be flapped up and caught beneath the roller or surcingle, so that whilst not being allowed to get cold, the animal is not overheated either.

Slipping rugs

Some horses and ponies keep their rugs in place very well, but those who roll a great deal, or have poor conformation, are less likely to do so, and this can cause problems such as sores, as well as the danger of getting cold.

If a rug slips persistently several things can be done.

55 Fitting a rug over a blanket

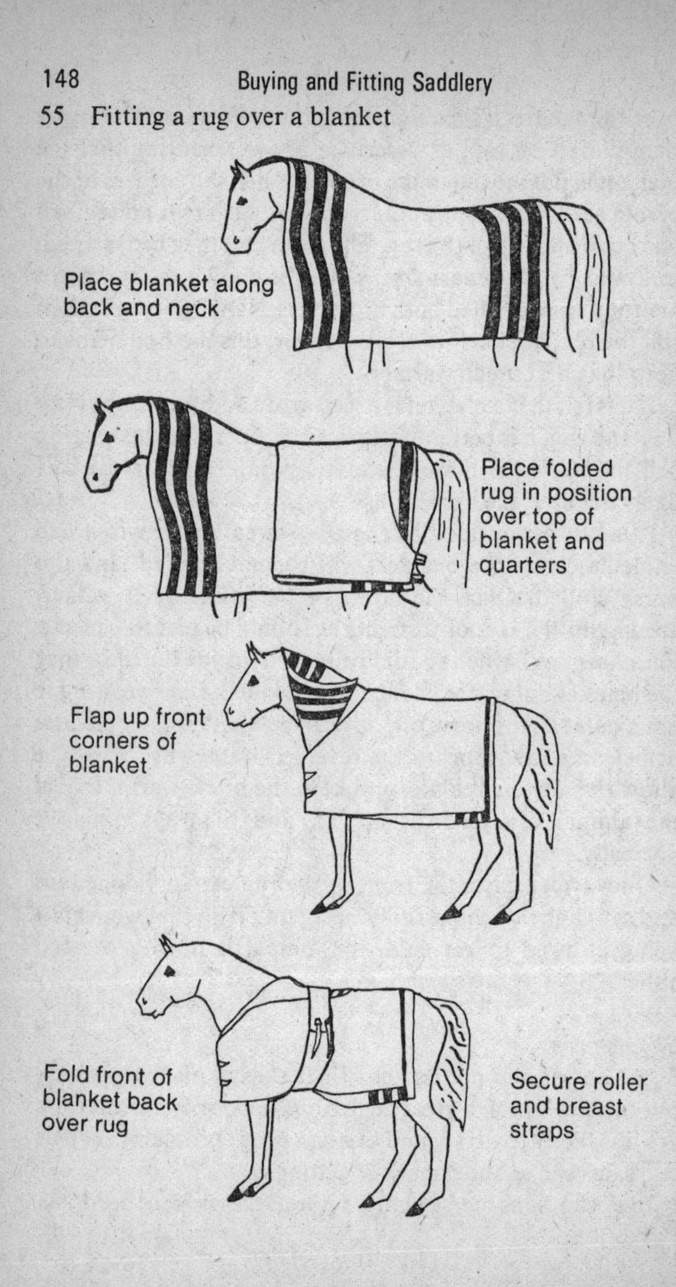

Firstly, all blankets and rugs should be put on so that they lie evenly to either side of the spine and so that the hairs of the coat lie flat. If the horse or pony is uncomfortable, it will fidget, causing the rugs to slip anyway. The roller or surcingle should be tight enough to keep the rugs on, but not so tight as to cause discomfort. A fillet string made of plaited strips of cotton or linen can also be added to loops stitched onto the back of the rug. The heavier and deeper the rug, the more likely it is to stay in place, especially if it has also been shaped around the quarters. On some brands of New Zealand rug, a drawstring is added, which makes it easier to mould it to the shape of the quarters.

When a roller is not sufficient to keep a rug in place, adding leg straps (if they are not already present) can sometimes offer a solution. If the rug always slips more to one side than the other, tightening the leg strap on the opposite side from that to which the ring slips more than the other will help prevent this. The traditional roller or surcingle is now beginning to give way to a system of belly straps, of which the methods of arrangement are many, but the purpose the same; to relieve spinal pressure. They also seem to be remarkably effective in maintaining the rug in the right place.

17

ROLLERS AND SURCINGLES

The traditional method of holding a rug in place is by fastening a roller or surcingle around both the rug and the horse. These can be made completely of leather (strong but rather expensive) or more frequently of a combination of webb or jute and leather. A rug should never be put on without a roller or surcingle, unless the front is left undone. It is better that the rug falls off than that it hangs around the animal's front legs and causes possible injury – not to mention damage to the rug itself.

56 A surcingle, a roller and an anti-cast roller

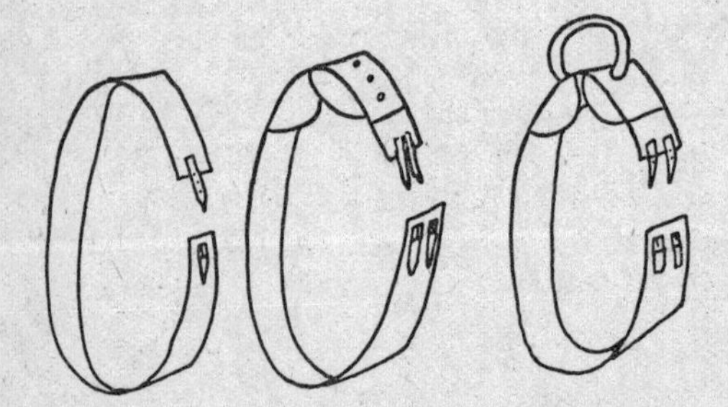

A roller differs from a surcingle in that it incorporates two padded pieces which rest on either side of the spine, and so prevent direct pressure on it. These padded sections are filled with foam or flock, and may need to be restuffed occasionally so that they carry out their function properly. As the surcingle lacks these pads, pressure on the spine from it can be considerable and damaging, so a thick piece of foam rubber or a knitted wither pad should be placed beneath it at the point where it crosses the backbone.

Both should be fastened quite firmly in order to hold the rug on, but not so tightly as a girth. Both forelegs should be pulled forward after fastening a roller or surcingle, so that pinching of loose skin around the elbow area does not occur. Both the buckles should be fastened at the same height, not on different holes; again this is to eliminate the danger of chafing. Traditionally, both are fastened on the near, or left-hand side.

With horses that roll, or have a habit of becoming 'cast' – that is to say, with their legs trapped against a wall so that they cannot get up, an anti-cast roller can prove a satisfactory solution. Most horses become cast because they try to roll right over, but the stable is not large enough to accommodate this. An anti-cast roller, made from leather, or leather and webb or jute has a metal hoop inserted into the section which passes over the back. The hoop thus prevents the horse from being able to roll right over.

Anti-cast rollers must be fitted as carefully as a saddle, since a badly fitting one can cause pinching, sores, and pressure points. To a degree, this problem can be overcome by buying a roller which is hinged, so that it is more likely to fit properly. An anti-cast roller should never be bought secondhand, since any damage which has occurred can often be difficult to spot, until the horse's back has actually been injured by it. Damage to such a roller is usually to the metal plates at both ends of the metal hoop; if they are at all warped or it is suspected that they have sustained damage, they should be taken immediately to a saddler and checked and repaired.

If the roller or surcingle tends to slip backwards, it can cause great panic, and the rug is likely to slip. This is most likely in animals with bad conformation, such as herring-gutted, or slab-sided, also in horses which are lean because they are fit.

To prevent this a breastplate made of webb or rugging can be attached to the roller or surcingle. Two 'D' rings for attachment will need to be added. The breastplate should be fastened so that it is a snug, not tight, fit.

18

INJURIES

Injuries frequently and unnecessarily arise from tack which fits badly, is misused, or is wrongly adjusted. They can also arise for other reasons so check not only the rider's own riding, but also for physical problems before rushing out to buy new saddlery. A horse may be uncomfortable in its mouth because it is teething, for example; this could lead to pulling at the bit and a sore mouth, which is neither the fault of the rider nor the tack, but simply a problem which will be grown out of.

Galls and Sores

One of the most common causes is dirty or unsupple tack. The best cure is prevention. New leather saddlery should be frequently oiled to make it as soft as possible and prevent any chafing. All tack should be kept clean, otherwise dirt between it and the skin will rub, causing soreness. The same applies to the horse or pony the tack is used on – if the animal is dirty, the same thing will happen.

All tack should be carefully examined when bought, to ensure that it fits properly, bearing in mind that an animal can often change shape if it loses or acquires fat or muscle, so that further regular checks should be made afterwards. New bridle leather stretches to a small degree in use.

Saddles should be checked and possibly restuffed (flocked up) every six months so that they do not begin to settle down and rub. It is possible for a saddle with a lot of flock in it to be very hard and rub the back, so sores are not always due to lack of flock – sometimes quite the opposite.

If the saddle has at some point become very wet, sometimes the flock inside will become lumpy, which will result in pressure points and sores. The rider's position should be checked for straightness, as crookedness and poor weight distribution can sometimes be a cause. Numnahs should always be pulled well up into the front arch of the saddle if used, so as to avert sore withers.

Both forelegs should be pulled forward after tightening the girth, so that no wrinkled skin is caught beneath it, causing painful pinching, and it should not be fastened too tightly or too loosely. The same applies when tightening a roller or surcingle; and, if a surcingle is used, a piece of foam should be placed beneath it where it crosses over the spine in order to avoid a sore back.

Sores sometimes occur when a horse or pony is wearing a rug for much of the time; most common are rubbed patches on the shoulders, withers, spine, and between the legs if legstraps are involved. Sores on the back can be dealt with by using a piece of foam as described above, or by resorting to a system of belly straps instead (see RUGS). Check that there is room enough for the shoulders to move comfortably without being restricted by the rug. If all is well there, pieces of real or synthetic sheepskin can be stitched into the lining along the affected area. This can also be done over the withers. Leg straps should be kept as clean as possible, and if made of leather, kept oiled and supple. If a great deal of chafing still occurs, then threading them through a piece of old bicycle inner tubing sometimes helps.

Any rug should always be removed and replaced at least twice a day, to minimise any danger of injury through slipping.

Saddle and girth sores can also be caused through an unfit

animal being worked too hard too soon, so time must be allowed in any fittening programme for the skin to harden in these areas.

Treatment

For any injury which involves broken skin, it is vital to make sure that the affected animal is covered against tetanus. The area can be bathed with warm salty water and then antiseptic cream or wound powder applied. If the skin has not been broken, then salty water can be used to bathe the region, which will also help to harden the skin. When riding an unfit horse, bathing the area with salty water or surgical spirits helps to harden the skin more quickly as a precaution anyway. Until the sore or gall has healed, all further pressure on it should be avoided, and riding ceased until it has gone.

Mouth injuries

These can happen through a badly fitting bit, a very soft mouth, or a rider with less than sympathetic hands. A worn or badly fitting bit can cut the tongue or lips, in which case a new one should be purchased, and use of any bit cease until the soreness has gone. Some horses and ponies do have very soft mouths, and it may be no fault of the rider or the bit if any injury arises. In this instance, a softer bit, such as a rubber, or rubber covered one, may prove to be the solution, or if necessary, a bitless bridle.

Treatment

Other than checking for protection against tetanus, and discontinuing the use of the bit until the area has healed, there is little that can be done, although obviously the cause should be remedied. A double handful of salt added to a water bucket will act as an antiseptic mouthwash. If the lips are cut, then an antiseptic cream applied will ease soreness and aid the natural healing process.

For sores at the corner of the mouth, a little Vaseline smeared on the edges of the mouthpiece helps to make it slide a little more easily, and less likely to injure.

Discoloured hair

When an injury has healed over, the hair usually grows through white afterwards. Regrowth of the hair can be encouraged by applying Vaseline, Cornucrescine, coconut oil, or a brand name of hair restorer; but once the hair has grown, the discolouration will remain. Sometimes horses with thoroughbred breeding will also develop a lighter shade of hair beneath the saddle. The different hair colouring should not be a worry, merely an indication of a possible past injury, and can be disguised for showing purposes as there are now a large range of hair tints in different shades which can be selected to match surrounding areas. A small test should be made first though, to check for possible adverse skin reactions.

INDEX

(References printed in **bold** type are main sections)